Heineken
AF593710

ISBN 0 333 36053 2 paperback
ISBN 0 333 36052 4 cased

First published 1983 by Macmillan London Limited. London and Basingstoke. Associated companies in Auckland, Dallas, Delhi, Dublin, Hong Kong, Johannesburg, Lagos, Manzini, Melbourne, Nairobi, New York, Singapore, Tokyo, Washington and Zaria.

Printed in Hong Kong.

THIRSTY WORK.

Ten years of Heineken Advertising.

Text: Peter Mayle

Design: Alan Waldie, Trevor Kennedy
Invaluable assistance: Sally Gutteridge

And the man who suggested this
book in the first place: Jamie Bryant.

"Promise, large promise,
is the soul of an advertisement."

——SAMUEL JOHNSON, 1758.——

MACMILLAN. LONDON.

Colin Millward

“Here we see the advertising writer at his labours.

Note the pensive gaze, the furrowed brow, the glass of inspiration close at hand.

Surely his creative muse will visit him soon.

But wait. All is not well.

The typewriter is silent. The shadowy figure of The Deadline lurks in the corner.

Clearly, our writer is in need of refreshment.”

1

"Gone to Marrakesh. Back soon."

Towards the end of 1973, Terry Lovelock (he of the pensive gaze and furrowed brow) was given the job of writing the advertising for Heineken lager.

The call was for something simple, persuasive, memorable and capable of infinite variation; something that would work on a beer mat or the screen of the Empire Leicester Square; something that would encourage hundreds of thousands of people to change their drinking habits. Something brilliant.

The creative brief – which is advertising language for all the information that the marketing and research people can provide about the product and the market, plus consumer trends, documented findings, informed guesses, wild speculation, bazaar gossip, conjectures, projections, summaries, suppositions, recommendations and directions – in the end, the creative brief was precise, if a little short. It was, in fact, the very briefest of briefs, and consisted of one word: *refreshment.*

Well, of course. Refreshment. Why else would you drink lager? How obvious it seems now. How obvious it was even in 1973. And yet there was a curious reluctance to let it anywhere near the advertising.

Back in those primitive days, the drinking of lager, although growing in popularity, was looked upon in much the same way that hang-gliding is today – an interesting pastime for other people, but not for the likes of you and me. You certainly weren't encouraged to drink lager for straightforward reasons like refreshment. The advertising of the time offered an interesting variety of inducements – drink lager if you want to be fashionable, drink lager if you like puns, drink lager if you run out of champagne, drink lager if you want to join an exclusive minority group. But drink lager for refreshment? How dull. How *ordinary.*

Nevertheless, that was what Lovelock was stuck with. The single word staring him in the face and time slipping by, marked only by a series of rejected ideas.

For most writers, the combination of a simple, clear brief and a deadline is one of the most unpleasant things in life. Once you admit that you understand and agree with the brief, there's no room for manoeuvre or gentlemanly negotiation. They've got you in a corner; you've got to produce.

And then you become aware of the office prowlers – those who hang around outside your office door, not wanting to pry, you understand, but on the spot just in case they might be needed to look at The Idea as it comes foaming out of your typewriter.

The effect of all this solicitous attention is that the mind becomes numb. Spasms of quiet desperation begin to squirt through the brain. The instinct is to escape the prowlers and run for the pub, pleading writer's block.

In this case, matters were made more than usually difficult because of the relationship between the client and the agency. Normally, it's a straightforward master/slave arrangement, with the client, depending on the mood of the moment, playing the part of Father Christmas or Attila the Hun, and the agency adjusting itself accordingly. But here, the situation was more complex – it was, in fact, a partnership. And more than that. Not only did the principals have a mutual respect for each other's professional abilities, but they liked each other. They enjoyed working together. They spent time together socially as *friends and equals.* Rare indeed!

Hardly surprising, therefore, that everyone concerned wanted to see more than just an adequate job done. And nobody wanted it more than Terry Lovelock, who by this time had spent eight weeks eyeball to eyeball with the one-word brief without once being interrupted by the ghost of an acceptable idea.

Even the prowlers outside his office had deserted him to prowl elsewhere. Did they know something he didn't know?

Put yourself for a moment in his place. Eight weeks with that one word. Eight weeks without a glimmer of inspiration. The blank, accusing sheet of paper in the typewriter. Your colleagues are being unusually tactful, and *not asking you* how it's going. What would you do?

Exactly! You'd go to Marrakesh for a week to straighten yourself out. One of the finer, more thickly marbled rooms in the Hotel Mamounia, picnics in the

Office prowlers, caught in the act.

Atlas mountains, fresh figs for breakfast, hot and cold running servants, a barman in a fez – if all that doesn't refresh a man's brain, nothing will. Pack your bags!

There is, however, a momentary hitch in the travel arrangements. On the morning of departure, Lovelock is supposed to be at a meeting with his Managing Director, Frank Lowe, who handles the Heineken account. (Advertising terminology is often faintly suggestive; people *handle* accounts and *service* clients. Sometimes vice versa.) The purpose of this meeting is to review the work that has been done, but at the appointed hour neither work nor writer can be found.

Somehow – maybe a note on Lovelock's desk saying "Gone to Marrakesh. Back soon" – Lowe's secretary manages to track down the fugitive at Heathrow airport and get him on the end of the phone.

The precise details of the exchange between Lowe and Lovelock are lost in the mists of time, but undoubtedly a few sharp words are passed, and there is a definite feeling of do or die about the conversation.

And it works! The whole thing sounds like the bad script of an implausible film, but this is

what happens: at three o'clock in the morning, Lovelock wakes in his room at the Hotel Mamounia, sits bolt upright, switches on the light, and scribbles with feverish hand:

Heineken refreshes the parts other beers cannot reach

Right! Where are you now, you office prowlers, when the real stuff is coming out? Three o'clock in the morning! Genius never sleeps!

□ □ □

Returning to London with his fez held high, Lovelock shows the idea to Frank Lowe in the form of several scripts for television commercials.

There are a few moments of silence while Lowe reads the scripts. A smile. "Yes. I like the line, and I like the piano tuner script. Try a few more, and let's see if it works on a poster."

That little misunderstanding at the airport is forgiven.

□ □ □

The next stage in the proceedings is the presentation of the idea to the client. This is traditionally an occasion when the agency puts on a performance which combines elements of Star Wars and Bertram Mills Circus in a setting reminiscent of a merchant bank boardroom. The trick is to dress up what is essentially a simple piece of communication in a way that will give if the weight of a sound commercial investment. Big money is at stake here, millions of pounds, and you don't get approval for that kind of expenditure with a scruffy bit of paper and a chat. No, sir. We're all *businessmen* here.

And so the agency boardroom is bedecked with inch-thick marketing documents and young men in dark suits (at least one young man for each visiting member of the client organisation). Charts and statistics are flashed up on the screen. Jingles are played at a volume just this side of brain damage. Commercials are unveiled. Evidence of effort comes bursting out of the walls. All that is missing is someone jumping out of a giant cake – that is, unless the client is a cake manufacturer.

At the end, as the last notes of the jingle die away for the umpteenth time, the agency people look expectantly at the client people, for all the world like cuckoos waiting for the worm. The focus of attention narrows down to the senior client – the man with the worm! – and all ranks lean forward attentively.

Mmm. Yes. Well. Most interesting. You've certainly

On the left, Lenin. On the right, Anthony Simonds-Gooding. Over the page, a trip to Russia.

given us a lot to think about. And with a gathering up of documents and a flurry of dark suits, the presentation ends. Drinks and anti-climax all round.

As it happens, the Heineken campaign (here comes that implausible script again) was presented to the client at an altitude of 20,000 feet in a Russian airliner. This was not a new and enterprising sales technique, but a consequence of the friendship between Frank Lowe and his client, Anthony Simonds-Gooding, the Marketing Director in charge of Heineken. The two friends – or perhaps we should call them comrades – had arranged to go to Leningrad together to visit the Hermitage museum.

The outing had been planned well in advance, in the confident expectation that the campaign would have been done long before Lowe and Simonds-Gooding headed for the buffalo grass vodka and the cultural delights of old Russia. A few days off from the cares of business, a modest pot of caviar to celebrate a job well done, and nothing to worry about except keeping your ears warm.

But there was, shall we say, a slight uneasiness in the air as the plane took off – a small cloud, no bigger than a pint mug. The agency had been working for several months on the problem without any visible results. Television time had been booked, and would be embarrassing and expensive to cancel. The first commercial was due to go on the air in a few weeks. The game was rapidly getting into injury time.

To his eternal credit, Simonds-Gooding had not once pressed the agency to show him something – anything, even the rejected ideas – until they were ready. But here we are on the plane with a couple of hours to kill and the subject is, after all, weighing heavily on the mind.

All right, Frank. Come on. What's happening?

Do the presentation on a plane? Well now, here's a change from jingles in the boardroom. In fairness, it should be said that both Lowe and Simonds-Gooding detest the Busby Berkely School of presentation. Even so, the facilities on Aeroflot Flight SU 638 are limited. If you can't write it down on the back of an air-sickness bag, there is nothing else available in the way of visual aid. It comes down to the power of speech and the strength of the idea.

Lowe goes through the reasoning which led to the one-word brief of refreshment. Fine. He delivers the immortal line and describes one of the commercials, which features a piano tuner's ear. It is not remotely like beer advertising. He finishes. Should he get off at Leningrad, or change for Siberia?

Relax. As Simonds-Gooding says, "it was love at first sight."

Lowe

THE METHOD BEHIND THE MADNESS

Of all the criticisms aimed at the Heineken campaign when it first appeared, perhaps the most weighty, the one which seemed to smack of great wisdom, the one that would be delivered with much shaking of the head and sucking of teeth, was that it was *too risky.*

What the critics overlooked was that the campaign, although unusual in its expression, was soundly based on one of the most fundamental principles of advertising, which is this:
if you can take the main benefit of the product category, *and make it the property of your brand,* you will have a massive and enduring advantage over your competitors.

The most important benefit, by a mile, that lager can offer is refreshment. Even ten years ago, everyone knew that; all the evidence was there. It was ignored or avoided, either because it seemed too obvious to be interesting, or too difficult to turn into distinctive advertising.

There was, as a result, an opportunity – provided you could make the advertising sufficiently compelling – to adopt the central benefit of lager, the generic commodity claim of refreshment, and make it yours.

And if you could add to that some reassurance about your brand's continental origins (because that's where genuine lagers come from) – well, then you would be doing the two most important jobs in the book.

With a base like that, which wouldn't date or become unfashionable, you could construct an advertising campaign with "legs" – something that would last for years. And obviously, if your advertising money, year after year, is spent on one strong idea, it is a much more effective way of doing business than changing your mind and your message every eighteen months.

The other advantage of a simple, soundly-based idea is that it encourages creative experimentation. You can afford to have some fun, which is where people often start talking about risk. In fact, really high-risk advertising is that bland, "safe" stuff with all the impact of faded wallpaper, invisible from birth, and destined to be a total waste of money.

□ □ □

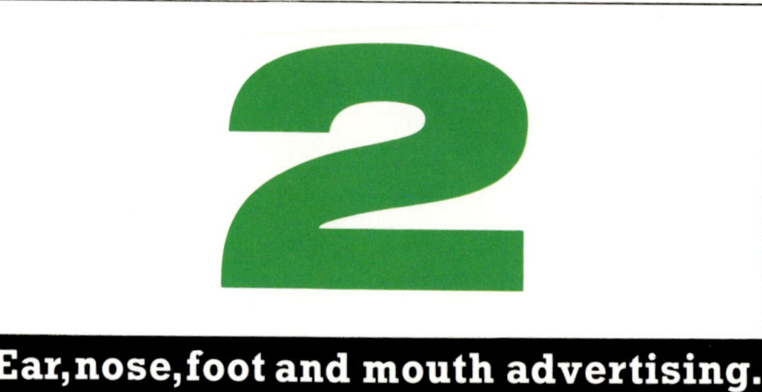

2

Ear, nose, foot and mouth advertising.

The critics and prophets of doom who circle round any conspicuous new advertising campaign, darting in from time to time to nip at its ankles, were more or less unanimous about the early Heineken work. It was not beer advertising. It was a biology lesson, and would doubtless meet a suitably anatomical end by falling flat on its face.

And looking back, yes, there *is* an emphasis on parts of the body – not the traditional, boys-will-be-boys parts of the body like right arms and the barmaid's cleavage, but unromantic appendages, extraordinary articulations, sometimes even bizarre contusions and deformities. Risky ground it must have seemed, and particularly in beer advertising. Because there are, as we shall see later, certain rules, certain comfortable conventions, certain boats you don't rock, certain sacred cows you worship. All these have been blatantly ignored from the first commercial onwards.

But we are ahead of ourselves. Let us go back and, in a calm and analytical manner, review the first two scripts and the first two posters.

What do we see? Ah, yes. A mildly deranged old piano tuner with defective hearing and, for all we know, a wooden leg and halitosis; a collection of feet – *nude* feet – belonging to policemen who have lost the ability to perform that most basic of constabulary duties, the policeman's bounce; a moustache which, if it were a dog, would have been put down; and a nose which appears to have lost any kind of interior skeletal support.

Not a pretty list. You will notice that an unwholesome preoccupation with physical infirmity runs through this catalogue of misery. But, we are told, help is at hand. Heineken is the remedy for perforated ear-drums, fallen arches, terminal moustache droop, and collapsed sinus passages.

Good grief! Doctors have had their stethoscopes confiscated and been horsewhipped down Harley Street for less extravagant claims than those. Surely this madness can't be allowed to run gibbering through the airwaves and into that holy place, the British living room?

Fortunately for all of us, there is one bastion of sanity and good taste which can be trusted to put the hoop on this kind of dangerous nonsense before it is unleashed on the public. It is the Independent Television Contractors Association, guardian of our delicate sensibilities, defender of common decency, dedicated foe of the Misleading Statement and the Unprovable Claim.

The ITCA, as it it known to its friends, is the filter through which every script and every commercial must pass before it is allowed on the air. The people who make up the approval committee are experienced, highly-trained, and capable of spotting a half-truth, an off-colour innuendo, or a suspect claim almost before it slips through the door. Does this dog food *really* contain significant amounts of marrowbone jelly? Can you *prove* that your detergent will remove those unsavoury stains from little Alan's T-shirt? The public must not be hoodwinked, and the ITCA is there to see that it isn't. Noble work!

And yet even Homer sometimes nods. Something is desperately awry here. Frank Lowe takes the campaign line – Heineken refreshes the parts other beers cannot reach – and those first two scripts – the piano tuner with defective hearing and the policemen with defective feet – he takes the entire preposterous and unprovable bundle to the elders of the ITCA. And what do they do?

They approve it.

□ □ □

The time has now come to press our noses up against the window of the film business, and watch in silent wonder as paper turns to celluloid and scripts become commercials.

The film business! The world of quick fame and the big lunch and those mystical, profoundly inspirational words, "off on location all expenses paid." Starlets and limousines and salami-sized cigars and *glamour.*

Well, not quite. The most enduring memory you will have after watching a commercial being shot is boredom, often accompanied by heartburn caused by bicep-shaped sausage sandwiches and over-stewed tea. A day on the set is a day of enormous tedium and considerable discomfort. You are not allowed to speak. You are frowned at if you move. You hold yourself unnaturally still, fighting off cramp, and peer towards the centre of activity in the hope of seeing something – perhaps not the soliloquy from Hamlet – but *something exciting.* After all, this is a distant cousin of show business.

Sound! Camera!
And... *Action!*

What you see is the same short sequence repeated forty-six times. The dialogue that you find amusing at ten o'clock is irritating by eleven and actively offensive by noon. And, more infuriating still, the last thirty-four takes all sound identical anyway. Why go through it again?

Because, unknown to an ignorant novice like you who doesn't know a whip pan from a lap dissolve, there is always some poor goon *doing something wrong.* This is never admitted as human fallibility. It is always the fault of a malevolent abstract force.

Take One: the actor delivers his lines superbly, but the sound engineer isn't happy with the level.

Take two: the actor delivers his lines superbly, the sound level is good, but the make-up girl notices that the actor's false nose is slipping.

Take three: the actor delivers his lines superbly, the sound level is good, the nose holds fast, but the product – our hero! – is sweating under the lights.

And so it goes on. And on. And on. There are frequent pauses for refreshment – the first morning tea break, elevenses, the early lunch break, the disturbed lunch break, the early afternoon tea break, the proper tea break, the pre-overtime break – and it is quite possible to eat badly five or six times in the course of the day. It is the proud boast of the ACTT – the film technicians' union – that it has never in its history lost a member through lack of nourishment.

The shooting day starts about eight in the morning, and never finishes before five or six in the evening. At the end of it, if it's been a good day, you have thirty or forty seconds of film and chronic indigestion. As someone once said, it is only slightly more exciting than waiting for Astroturf to grow. Nevertheless, duty must be done! Let casting commence for batty old piano tuners and policemen's feet.

The film production company, under the direction of Vernon Howe, shoots the first two commercials. They are edited, the sound track is added, optical effects are inserted – all those mysterious processes that take place in poky premises in Soho – and by the time the first film is finally in the can and ready for public consumption, there is precisely one week until the first transmission on television.

Just made it under the wire! Except for one final and, it must be said with fingers crossed, crucial approval. The proprietor – the owner of the name, the brewer of the beer, Monsieur le Patron, Mr. Heineken himself – he has yet to see the commercials.

Anthony Simonds-Gooding shows them to Freddie Heineken, and again we have an example of man's eternal optimism and trust in his fellow man. It is a replay of the earlier presentation.

Approved! Let's get the little rascals on the air and see what happens.

□ □ □

Advertising differs from most other forms of mass communication in one important respect: people are reluctant to admit that they are influenced by it. *Advertising is not a socially acceptable stimulus.*

It's quite acceptable to admit the influence of a film or a TV programme or a book or a newspaper. It is sometimes even considered fashionable to be influenced by those walking examples of mass communication such as the Princess of Wales, tennis players, footballers and pop singers. But advertising – which we are all exposed to in one form or another every day, which has billions of pounds spent on it, which comes at us from every angle and on every kind of surface from book matches to marathon runners' backsides – advertising does not impinge on the normal, intelligent adult's life.

Or so they are fond of saying. Never! Not me! I am the master of my ship and nobody – not even Captain Birds Eye – is going to tell *me* what to have for dinner.

Of course. Obviously. Who likes to admit that they are somehow being, dare we say it, manipulated? But whether it's admitted, or buried in the psyche along with all that other dark inadmissible stuff, the fact is that advertising *does* sometimes influence people's decisions. And the clear, incontrovertible proof of that is when you change your advertising campaign and the sales go up. It is, of course, equally possible to change your advertising and see sales go down. But either way, there is a problem: the effects are not immediately apparent. Overnight, nothing happens. It takes weeks, often months, before you know whether you're doing something right or something wrong.

This period of uncertainty imposes a considerable strain on the patience of all concerned. The budget is being spent, the advertising is pumping out, but there's no reaction. You might as well be tossing the money in the Thames for all the good it seems to be doing. And you're not asking for much. All you want is the answer to one simple question: do they – the punters whom you're trying to reach with your advertising at such vast expense – do they like it? Because if they like it, there's a good chance they'll buy what you're selling. (This theory, which seems

plain and reasonable, is regarded with profound suspicion by some companies. They believe that, given enough money and noise, you can stun the public into buying anything. Their commercials are strident, often illiterate, and always disagreeable, frequently set to something that masquerades as music.)

Well, enough of theorising. Let's have some hard news. Are we getting through to them or aren't we? A few weeks of this suspense is more than flesh and blood can stand. One day, something snaps in the corporate central nervous system. We must have some information! And if the public won't come to us, then we shall have to go to them. Summon the soothsayers and witch doctors (who prefer to be called Attitude and Opinion Research Executives), and let's get down on the street or in the grass roots or wherever it is they're all hiding, and let's find out *what the people think.*

So you round up what is known as a "significant sample" and get to work on them. In essence, although the questions will be couched in terms of immense subtlety and cunning, what you want to know is: Have you seen my advertising, and what do you think of it? Brace yourself. The people who make up your significant sample will now offer you a series of statements which may flatly contradict each other. First, they will say that they are barely aware of any advertising, let alone yours, and wouldn't dream of paying attention to it anyway. When pressed for an opinion about your advertising, they will compare it – unfavourably, and in great detail – with the competitive advertising they have just told you they haven't seen. The more novel your idea, the more it differs from existing advertising in that category, the more unexpected it is, the worse the research results are likely to be.

When the Heineken campaign was researched, response was mixed; it was either bad or terrible. A common complaint cropped up again and again – *it's not proper beer advertising.* Where are those chaps in pubs having a good time? Where is the barmaid? Where is the obligatory worship of the pint pot? Where is the jovial host with a cheery word for all? Get out of here with your piano tuners and policemen! *It's not proper beer advertising.*

There is only one thing to do when faced with a research document which disagrees so fundamentally and catastrophically with your deeply-held beliefs and professional instincts, and after a short discussion, Simonds-Gooding and Lowe agreed to do it.

The research was ignored.

THREE MEN IN A PUB, AND OTHER GOLDEN RULES

In 1973, there were a number of commandments which dictated the structure and content of almost every beer commercial. Not necessarily in order of importance, they were:

1. All commercials shall be shot in pubs.

2. There shall be three principal characters in each commercial – Eric, Derek, and their mate Jack.

3. Each commercial shall show a friendly confrontation. Eric and Derek will gang up against Jack. Or sometimes Jack and Eric will gang up against Derek. The formation of the teams is not important. What is important is that one of the three is obliged to buy pints for the others. He will then have his back slapped, and there will be manly laughter.

4. The act of drinking shall at all times be preceded by a moment of glassy-eyed reverence, of discovery almost, as if nothing quite as beautiful has ever been seen in a glass before. The act of drinking shall be followed by a brief period with the eyes half-closed, and the mouth shall be composed in an expression of purest joy. At no time will bystanders show any surprise or concern at this demented behaviour.

5. The landlord shall be large and relentlessly jolly. He will watch the antics of Eric, Derek, and Jack with amused tolerance, occasionally cocking an eyebrow conspiratorially at the camera.

6. Women shall, from time to time, be permitted to take part as long as they pose no threat to the camaraderie of Eric, Derek, and Jack. For safety's sake, it is recommended that women shall be tucked away behind the bar. This also makes it possible to include both a handsome bosom *and* a pint in the final shot.

Funnily enough, when you look at beer commercials today, ten years later, it is as if time has stood still. Eric, Derek, and their mate Jack – with different haircuts – are *still there.*

□ □ □

WHAT A DREADFUL CAMPAIGN; LET'S GIVE IT A PRIZE

Every year, the Designers & Art Directors Association, in its infinite wisdom, gives awards for outstanding work. These awards are the advertising industry's Oscars. In its first year, the Heineken advertising failed even to qualify. In its second year, it won the gold award for exactly the same campaign that had been thrown out the year before.

This is one small indication of the innately conservative nature of the advertising man, who will always check to see that the bandwagon is actually moving before he jumps on it.

□ □ □

"NOT THE SORT OF THING YOU'D LIKE TO SEE WHEN YOU'RE EATING YOUR TEA."

Some time after the first commercials appeared, 30 beer drinkers (the legendary "significant sample") were asked what they thought of the advertising.

Nobody anticipated rapturous applause. When confronted with a novel idea, or a novel form of expression, most people instinctively take refuge in attitudes that have been formed by existing ideas. If the new idea doesn't fit in (and if it's new, it won't) then it will get bad marks.

Nevertheless, the first Heineken reviews were notable for their lack of kindness. For instance:

"Blatant untruth"

1973

"The commercials are lacking in impact, punch, or motivating power"

"The slogan doesn't stick. No rhythm about it"

"They wouldn't increase sales here"

"What's beer got to do with ears?"

"It's not very funny, so they must expect me to believe it"

"It's a lie!"

"Nothing to do with beer"

"It's meant to be a doctor's prescription"

"Feet and beer put me off"

"Silly"

"Not the sort of thing you'd like to see when you're eating your tea"

Not wanting to be left out, the research company ventured an opinion too:

"It is considered that, overall, the commercials are unlikely to promote aware ness of Heineken and interest in drinking it."

□ □ □

The Great Dane.

Oh, the agony that goes into choosing voices for commercials! The hours of deliberation, of listening to tapes, of becoming immersed in tiny but critical details like aspirated aitches, nasal vowels, glottal stops, breath suppression – the *vital nuances.* And then there is the overall impression to consider, the personality of the voice. Is this – and here we quote a television producer with no control over her metaphors – is this the kind of voice that comes up to you with a smile on its face and puts its arm round your shoulder?

You see? It isn't just a simple matter of dragging in some actor who is resting between engagements. The voice has to be right. Otherwise the commercial will be like a beautiful girl who screeches – you may enjoy looking, but you won't want to listen.

There is also, in the case of Heineken, the delicate question of what is known in brewing circles as the *continental heritage.* Lager beer was invented in Europe, and despite the EEC, the *Entente Cordiale,* day trips to Ostende and all the rest of it, Europe – "The Continent" – remains forever foreign. This is usually associated with grave disadvantages like garlic and the inability to speak proper English, but when it comes to lager, there is a softening in our attitudes. Indeed, one might almost say that a lager isn't really a lager unless it has its roots in the continent.

All of which adds to the problem of finding the right voice. We're advertising a *faintly foreign* product here, and it's no use having a warm, sympathetic, expressive, impeccably modulated voice with a Yorkshire accent. A lager from Barnsley would be, somehow, unconvincing.

Right. So we're looking for a friendly, persuasive voice with a sense of humour (how can you be serious about policemen's feet?), but with a certain exotic quality – not definitely Scandinavian, not definitely Dutch, not definitely Bavarian, but definitely *continental.*

A fair description, now we come to look at it, of the voice of Victor Borge.

□ □ □

Every advertising writer should be lucky enough, once in his working life, to have a script recorded by Borge. The man has a marvellous gift for taking a modestly amusing line and making it sound better, more witty, than it has any right to expect. A lot of this, probably most of it, comes from timing and delivery. But there is something else as well – Borge has a thorough understanding of advertising and selling which is unusual, to say the least, among graduates of the Copenhagen Music Conservatory.

Well now, how did this come about? What have we here? A misspent youth as an advertising executive? Creeping off after piano practice to study sales figures and research documents?

Almost. Because there were a few hectic years in Victor Borge's life when, in addition to his duties on the stage and at the keyboard, he was a one-man advertising agency *and* client combined. He was manufacturer, production manager, sales director, advertising writer, company spokesman, and treasurer of his own enterprise. Yes, ladies and gentlemen, it is our great pleasure to present to you, fresh from the Borge farm, that delightful creature, short of leg and plump of breast, the Rock Cornish hen!

Virtually single-handed, Borge was responsible for introducing Rock Cornish hens to America. He bred them on his farm, promoted them on his radio shows, during his stage performances, in interviews – wherever he went, which was all over America, the Rock Cornish hen was sure to follow. And, because the public liked Borge, they were prepared to try his hens. The power of testimonial advertising! Buying hens from a pianist is about as logical as buying a piano from a chicken farmer, but there we are. It happened.

In the end, hen business began to interfere with show business. The orders, and the amounts of money

needed for expansion, became so enormous that Borge found more and more that he was working for the birds. So he stopped, closed down the business, and with his place in Rock Cornish hen history assured, went back to being a full-time entertainer.

The advertising lessons learned during what we might call his fowl period have stayed with Borge ever since. He knows that in the right hands, or coming out of the right mouth, advertising works. As a result, he has been remarkably selective over the years about the advertising that he takes on, and insists on the right of script approval.

It is against this background that we meet Borge's agent, Tito Burns, who has just received several Heineken scripts together with the suggestion that Borge might like to record them.

No, he wouldn't. He has nothing against the scripts, but he's very busy, he lives three thousand miles away from the agency, and anyway, if he were going to give his all for a beer, it would be a Danish beer.

And now, as in any improbable tale, Destiny makes an appearance, in the shape of none other than Orson Welles.

Just as the matter of the scripts is about to be closed, Tito Burns, with a finely judged sense of timing, mentions this little piece of theatrical gossip: not that it's of any special interest to you Victor, but I hear that your friend Orson Wells is going to be the voice for all the Carlsberg advertising.

Mischievous work, Tito! How can you say a thing like that to a Dane about a Danish beer? Orson Welles, indeed! Magnificent actor, man of genius and charming fellow no doubt, but when all's said and done, he's *not Danish.* How do you expect a good Dane to take that kind of news?

"Give me the scripts, Tito. I'll do them."

And he did.

THE JOYS OF RECORDING (MERDE ALORS!) IN FRANCE.

Lowe and Borge.

At 9.30 one morning in the south of France, two groups converge from different directions on a small recording studio in an otherwise respectable part of Nice.

From the west, clutching scripts and the roughly edited version of a recently shot commercial, come the people from the advertising agency. From the east, the direction of Monte Carlo, come Victor Borge and Tito Burns.

The purpose of the meeting is to record the scripts of two television commercials and some experimental radio commercials, and you may well ask why serious and important work like this has to be tackled amid the distractions of the Cote d'Azur. What's wrong with one of those poky little places in Soho?

The reason is – let's give credit where it's due – the reason is the agency's regard for the well-being of the artist. Borge, who is normally either in Connecticut or the Caribbean, happens to be in Monte Carlo to give a concert for the crowned heads of the media business. Well, the poor man has enough on his plate already; we can't ask him to come over to London. No, it's up to us to do the decent thing and meet him in France. Duty calls!

So here we are, 9.30 in the morning, in the studio, which is decorated with a living mural of young Frenchmen drinking coffee and clearing their throats in a significant fashion. Surely they can't all be sound engineers? We do have the *chef du son,* Jean-Jacques, here at the control panel, and his arms seem long enough to reach all the buttons and switches without any help. Who are these others? What is their function?

Never mind. The studio looks quite adequate – clean and well-lighted, and there is even a piano. Borge sits down and flexes his arpeggios while Jean-Jacques toys with the control panel. The other young men – Jean-Claude, Jean-Pierre, Jean-Luc, and Jean-Francois – busy themselves getting coffee and (you can tell we're in foreign parts) beer. They then arrange themselves gracefully against the wall.

Bon. Allons-y. Borge is ready, Jean-Jacques is ready. Let us roll.

After a few takes, Borge comes out with a particularly good reading. Excellent. Can we hear that one again, Jean-Jacques?

Comment?

Play it back. *Encore une fois.*

Ah, oui.

Knobs are twiddled, fingers fly over the console, and the playback switch is activated.

But all is not well. Instead of Victor Borge reading a Heineken script, we hear the stirring sounds of a military march and a man's voice inviting us to visit a local supermarket. Somehow or other, Radio Monte Carlo is being broadcast through the feedback system.

Merde alors! Jean-Jacques pushes and pulls and twiddles furiously, cutting off all communication between the control room and the recording studio. Borge, now sealed off completely from the outside world and unaware of this technical hitch, can be heard very faintly asking if anybody is still there.

The young men look on anxiously as Jean-Jacques goes through his entire repertoire of sockets and jack-plugs until – *voilà!* – normal service is resumed, and we can hear the reading again.

Half an hour and a couple of scripts later, all is going suspiciously well. Borge, in fine form, is giving us a dozen variations for each script. Jean-Jacques and his supporters club have started to relax. Lulled into a false sense of normality, we ask if the next reading could be done with an echo effect.

Comment?

Could we have some echo?

Mais oui. Jean-Jacques barks at one of the young men, who leaves the room at speed. Where could he be going? Is echo kept in the studio basement? In a shop round the corner?

The young man returns in triumph, with half a dozen bottles of beer. *Voilà!* He beams.

Ah well. You can always put echo on in London.

□ □ □

Borge and his agent, Tito Burns.

A commercial break.

It comes as a surprise to many people that *real* film directors – the kind who have agents in Los Angeles and dinner with Woody Allen and Christmas cards from David Puttnam – would even consider directing commercials. Imagine the contrast! The dizzy drop in dramatic content!

Here is our feature film director, fresh from coaxing the performance of the century out of some mythical figure like Alec Guinness, his mind still savouring the creative cut and thrust of directing a Great Actor, eager for the next challenge. And – too late to duck now! – here it comes:

We open on an establishing shot of a bright, modern kitchen. Two young housewives are comparing soiled clothes…

Over to you, Mr. Hollywood! Make something out of *that* before you go off for drinks with Dino de Laurentiis.

All right – maybe a good director wouldn't touch a commercial like that unless the alimony payments really had him by the throat, but there is a lot of serious talent around directing 40-second epics, and it can't be just the money.

In fact, the director's fee – "I'm sure we won't fall out over money" – isn't the incentive. What feature directors love about commercials is the abundance of time and the generosity of the production budgets. Instead of breaking your neck to get five or ten minutes of film shot in one day, all you have to worry about is thirty or forty seconds. You want to do another take? Go ahead!

And the money which is available for "production values," for props, for all those wonderful barely-seen but vital touches that make set designers moan with pleasure – *the money's there.*

It's not easy nowadays to devise a half-minute commercial that can be shot for less than thirty thousand pounds. Fifty thousand is probably closer to the mark, and anything remotely complicated will go into six figures. Compare this rate – an average of around two thousand pounds per second of film – with the kind of money available on most feature films, and you can

understand why a director is strangely attracted to the prospect of a good commercial. He can make a marvellously polished film, a sumptuous offering, a small but perfect thing – just as long as you don't expect him to do it with those two insane housewives and their dirty linen.

Heineken has been lucky with directors, and vice versa. Here is a selection of commercials produced over the past ten years, and one mystery script as yet unshot.

□ □ □

A perplexed Alan Parker.

"Policemen's Feet"
1974 March

VICTOR BORGE:
In this simple experiment, we examine the effect of beer on the feet...

Now these feet have been walking all day and are very tired... We see that there is no movement in them ...which is due to lack of refresh ment.

So we adminster the cold Heineken...

Wait a few seconds...

and we observe that the Heineken is already refreshing the feet... causing lively movement of the toes and activating the arches.

Heineken is the only beer able to do this..

Because it refreshes the parts other beers cannot reach.

Jimmy Wormser.

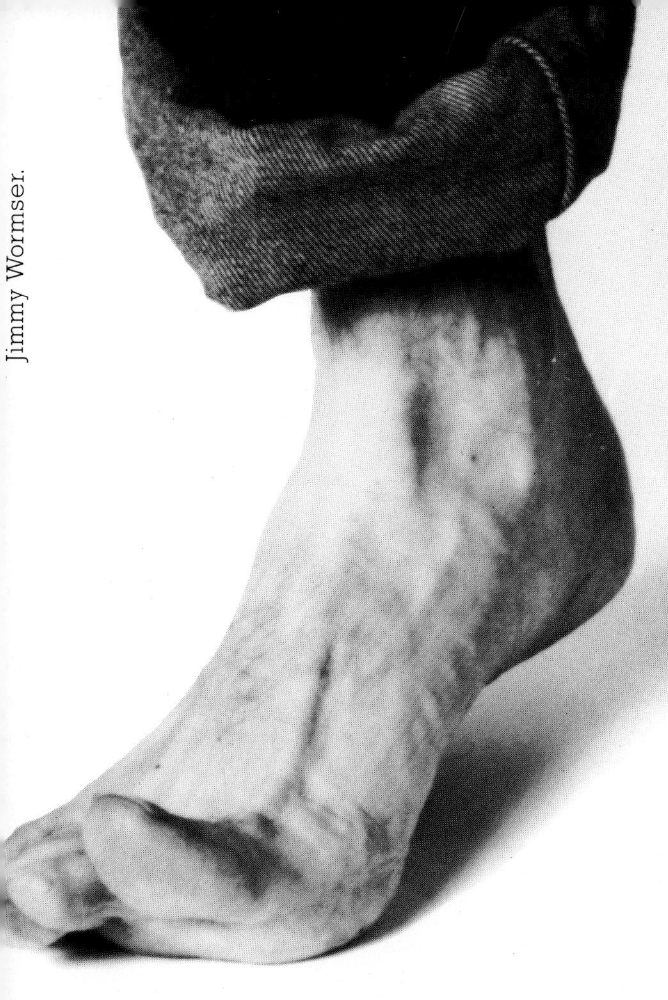

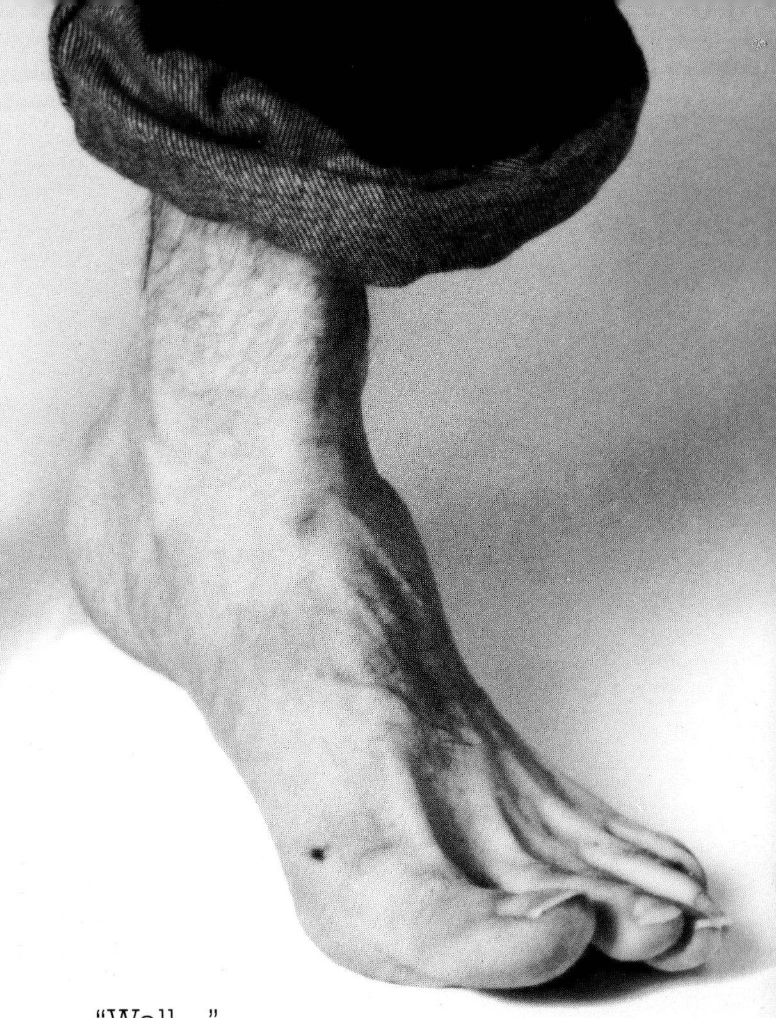

"POLICEMEN'S FEET"

The casting session, with director Vernon Howe in charge, begins.

"Good morning. Sit down and take off your shoes and socks."

"What?"

"We'd like to see the feet, if you don't mind."

"But I'm an actor. My agent didn't say anything about undressing."

"It's only the feet we want to see. There. We'll just take a Polaroid of them."

"Well..."

"They're perfect."

"They are?"

"Yes, it's those bunions and the tucked-in little toes. They're really ugly. Wonderful! Can you wiggle them for us? Terrific! Are you free next Tuesday?"

"Is any acting ability required?"

"Oh yes. Your feet will have to be very... *expressive.*"

"That's all right then. See you next Tuesday."

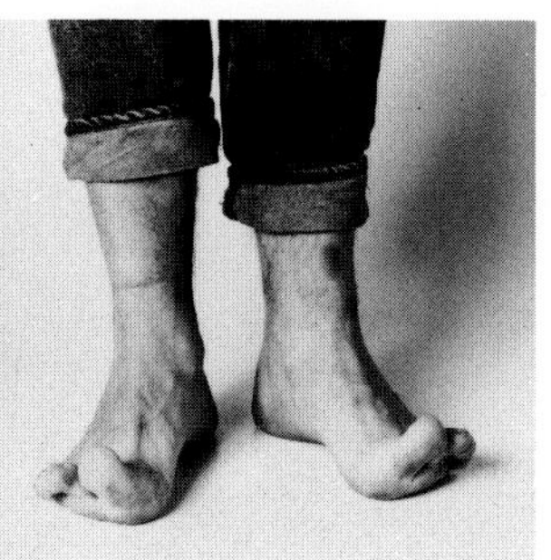

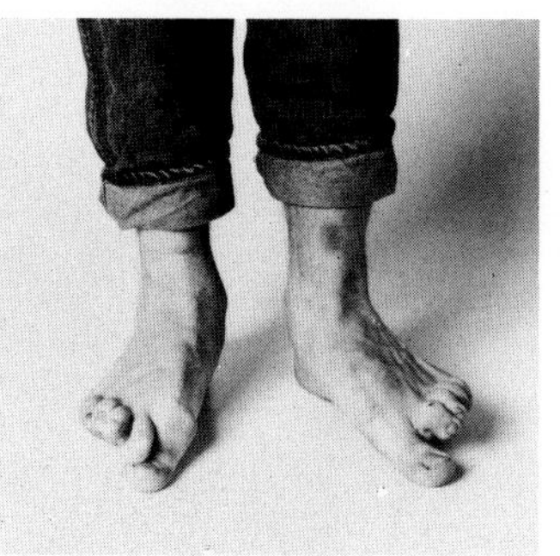

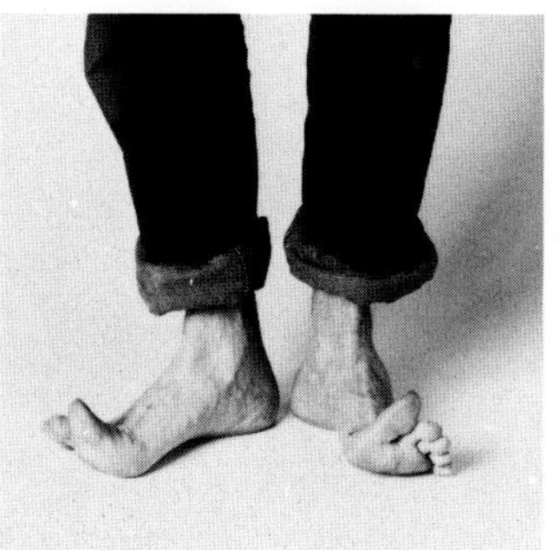

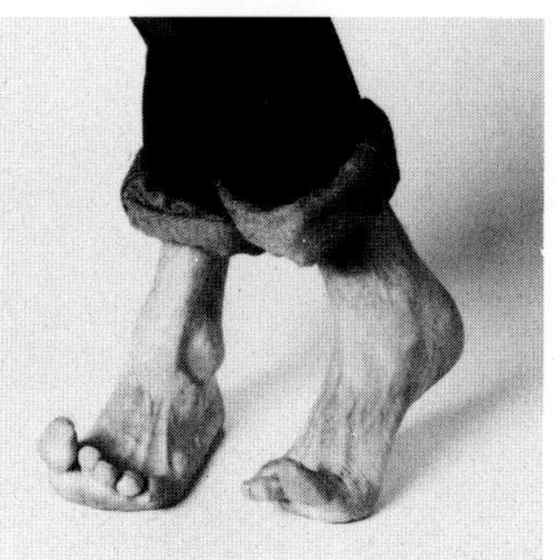

'Scrooge'

1974 November

This Christmas . . . things are not as they should be . . .

SFX:
Bells and carol singers in background.

The normally gasping fingers of Scrooge are nimbly tying presents . . .

There is obviously a lack of refreshment to Scrooge's traditional meanness . . .

SFX:
Moaning and clanking of chains in background.

Disturbed by this . . . the ghost of Jacob Marley has brought home a whole can of Heineken.

a little of which he gives to his partner . . .

and we see Heineken rapidly refreshing Scrooge's meanness . . .

enabling him to enjoy his Christmas in the old familiar way . . .

only Heineken is able to do this . . .

Because it refreshes the parts other beers cannot reach.

"SCROOGE"

Vernon Howe and Jacob Marley.

Once in a while, advertising is produced as a result of passionate and deeply-held personal convictions. This commercial is a case in point.

It is, as you will see, a celebration of meanness, and it was devised by two men whose wallets very rarely see the light of day: Terry Lovelock and Alan Waldie.

Between them, they transformed simple stinginess into an art form, and nowhere was the art more mercilessly practised than in restaurants. The reluctant host, he whose turn it was to pay, would pass secret instructions to the waiter ("Tell my friend the Bollinger's out of stock and there's no more smoked salmon"); the guest would feel obliged to visit the kitchen to make sure his order hadn't been replaced by a cheaper dish. And so it went on, with no quarter asked or given.

Terry Lovelock and Alan Waldie.

But one day, due to pressure of work and a temporary attack of generosity on both sides, a truce was called. Champagne was ordered while the problem at hand – a Christmas commercial for Heineken – was considered.

Let's see now. Something seasonal, obviously. Something that captures the essential spirit of the occasion. Something that adds a personal flavour to the traditional Christmas greeting – a symbol that reflects all those festive sentiments that Lovelock and Waldie hold most dear.

Yes. Exactly. Scrooge.

□ □ □

'Nero'
1976 April

VICTOR BORGE:
Ladies and gentlemen, after two weeks of continually watching the games...

the Emperor Nero is unable to decide the fate of the contestants ...this is because his thumb is exhausted.

SFX:
Expectant crowd noise.

After trying various remedies, his physicians conclude that Nero's thumb needs immediate refreshment...

So, the cold Heineken is ordered...

SFX:
Elaborate fanfare.

...of course with the minimum of fuss...

...and we see, how speedily Heineken refreshes this important part of the Emperor...

SFX:
Roar of crowd.

...enabling him to enjoy himself as only an Emperor can...

SFX:
Bigger roar from crowd.

...only Heineken can do this... because it refreshes the parts other beers cannot reach.

□ □ □

"NERO"

At the time it was shot, in April 1976, this was the most expensive commercial ever made in England. But look what you got for your money in those days: an epic!

Bob Brooks, the director, had an amphitheatre built in Shepperton Studios, with a special box, well removed from the cheap seats, to accommodate the noble court of Rome. There were standards, purple bunting and Imperial flags by the mile; togas and tin uniforms for 150 friends, Romans and spear-carriers; *and* – who can look upon him even now without a shudder! – the most evil, wet-lipped, degenerate Nero ever to come out of a Soho casting office.

So good was his performance – so perfectly debauched, so thoroughly nasty, clearly relishing the thought of tossing a few Christians to the lions – that he inspired swift and emphatic reations. The broadcasting authority (our old friends the ITCA) began to receive complaints from the public protesting at what they called "the ritual murder of Christians," and asking for Nero to be sent off for unsportsmanlike behaviour. The

commercial was promptly banned. The landslide of public opinion that caused the ban consisted of precisely six letters.

Fortunately, someone at the BBC saw the commercial before it was taken off the air, and asked the actor, Christopher Biggins, to play Nero (minus the cold Heineken) in *I, Claudius,* which he duly did.

His performance in *I, Claudius* was generally acknowledged to be superb, except for a tendency, spotted by one critic, for his thumb to twitch downwards at opening time.

□ □ □

'Most Successful Man'

1976 July

VICTOR BORGE
Today we are privileged to visit the most exclusive part of the South of France...where we find the world's most successful man...

a man who has everything...

a superb house...

the most beautiful women to attend him...

the latest yacht...

his personal helicopter...

yet...he is bored and dispirited...
life for him is totally lacking refreshment.

So, instead of the usual Champagne ...his butler serves him the cold Heineken.
But unfortunately, even the Heineken fails to refresh him...

A sad story...but let us all remember ...it is better to be a refreshed failure, than an unrefreshed success...

This sobering thought is brought to you from Heineken, the beer that refreshes the parts other beers cannot reach...usually.

□ □ □

Heineken. Refreshes the parts other beers cannot reach.

"MOST SUCCESSFUL MAN"

In the garden of a villa on Cap d'Antibes, the world's most successful man, played by Victor Borge, is awaiting instructions from the director, Ross Cramer. This is to be a scene filled with delicate shades of meaning, requiring immense concentration. The crew is silent. The Mediterranean is hushed in expectation.

And then – who *are* those people? – everything stops because the neighbours (if one can have such mundane things as neighbours on Cap d'Antibes) are having a boisterous lunch, and the sounds of revelry are distracting the dramatic scene in progress. How can we work with this going on? *Do something!*

There is a method for coping with situations like this. The director tells the assistant director to instruct the second assistant to sort it out. Offer the people champagne, invite them to watch the shoot, do whatever you want as long as you *keep them quiet.*

Five minutes pass. There is an urgent message for Ross Cramer. Could he join the agency people in their temporary office, which is a speedboat moored in the shallows?

Disregard the sunhats and rolled-up trousers; this is serious. The problem is that the neighbours – the boisterous lunchers – are Mr. Freddie Heineken, his family and friends. He owns the house next door, and he is on holiday. Why shouldn't he have lunch?

After some discussion, an elegant solution presents itself: filming will end for the day, to be resumed at 6.30 the next morning. All those neighbours who are up at that time are cordially invited to attend.

The next day, filming is finished well before lunch.

□ □ □

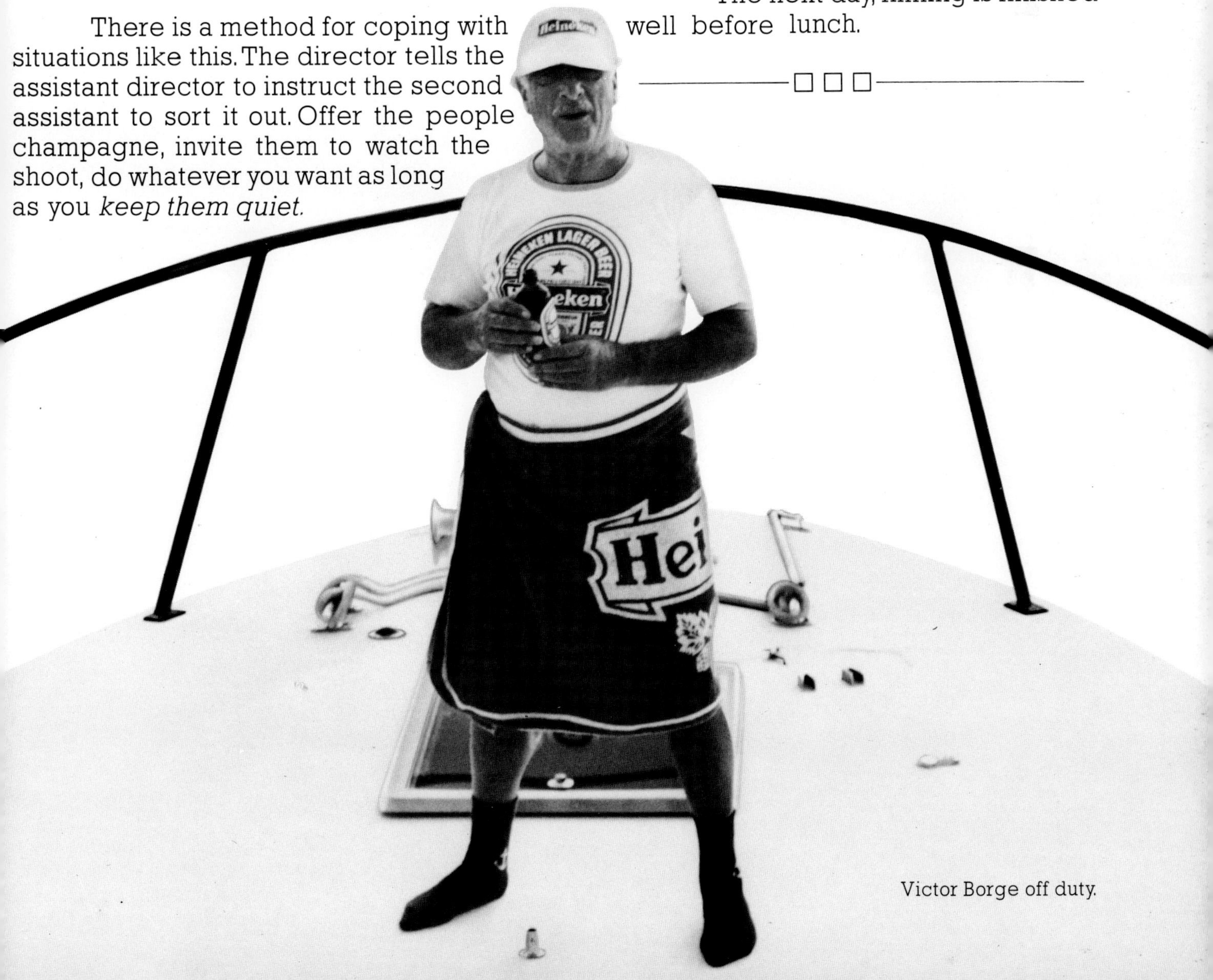

Victor Borge off duty.

'Galley'

1979 March

VICTOR BORGE:
We have received a number of letters – mainly we imagine, from non-beer drinkers – who doubt that Heineken refreshes the parts other beers cannot reach.

So we have devised this simple test to prove the Heineken claim.

All the men, as you can see, are totally exhausted after taking Ceasar water-skiing this morning... there is not a spark of refreshment in any of them.

So, we give those on the left the cold Heineken... and those on the right a selection of other beers, popular at the time.

Then we strike up the band...

...and immediately the Heineken has the desired effect on the rowers, if not on the boat.

CAESAR'S ASSISTANT
Stop, stop. We're going round in circles.

VICTOR BORGE:
Providing we believe, conclusive evidence that Heineken truly refreshes the parts other beers cannot reach.

□ □ □

"GALLEY"

How ridiculous. Here we have Alan Parker, director of "Bugsy Malone" and "Midnight Express," and one of the most inventive minds in the advertising business (close to genius, his Auntie Dolly says), and he's stuck. It's no good. There's no way round it. This commercial is going to end up costing three hundred thousand pounds. Minimum!

Let's go over it again. There's travel, board and lodging for two dozen large slaves (and you know how they eat); a galley will have to be built for them to row; we must have a helicopter; and then there's the hire of a large patch of the Mediterranean. Who said three hundred thousand? Closer to three and a half.

The point is that this is a classic demonstration, inspired by those marvels of mindless clarity, the washing powder commercials. Half the slaves are given Heineken; half are given ordinary lager. The Heineken oarsmen outpull their less refreshed colleagues.

Result: the boat goes round in circles.

You see the crux of it all? Unless everyone knows that the galley is going round in circles, the commercial doesn't work. Hence the helicopter, the Mediterranean, the galley, the complications – and the three hundred thousand pounds. Well, it's out of the question. A nice idea, boys, but not at that price.

Finally, Parker's producer, Alan Marshall, looks up from his copy of the Financial Times. With the weary air of a father addressing obtuse children, he says: "Why don't you get someone to say, 'We're going round in circles'?"

And with no further need for helicopters or galleys or even water, the commercial is shot indoors on the sound stage at Shepperton studios.

□ □ □

Alan Parker.

'Electric Tennis'

1980 March

SFX:
Electronic bleep of tennis ball as it bounces across the screen.

SFX:
Electronic bleep as glass appears on screen. Electronic glug of beer going into bat.

SFX:
Sound of electronic ball speeding across screen.

SFX:
Electronic bleeps to punctuate words as they appear on screen.

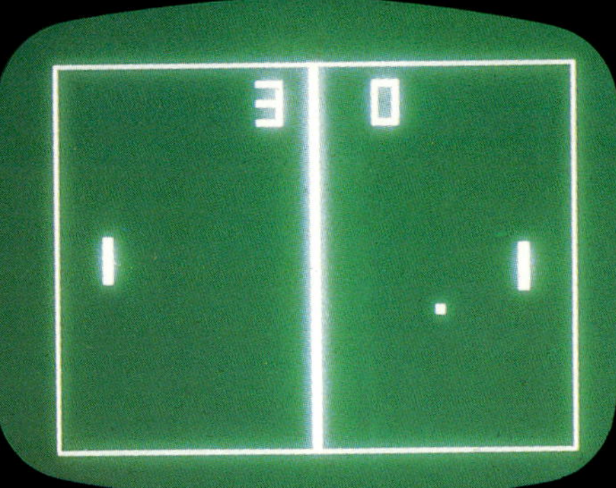

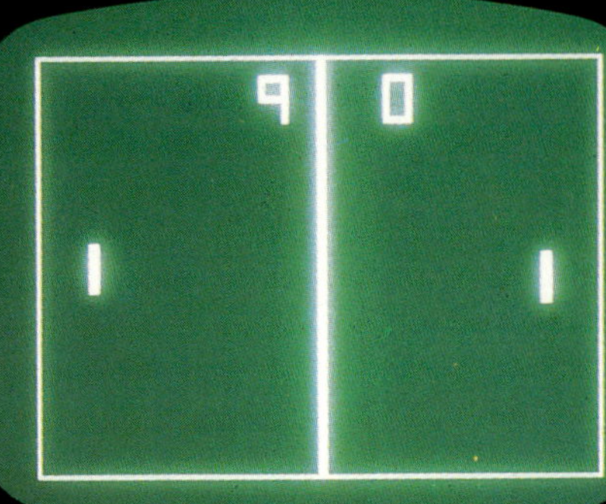

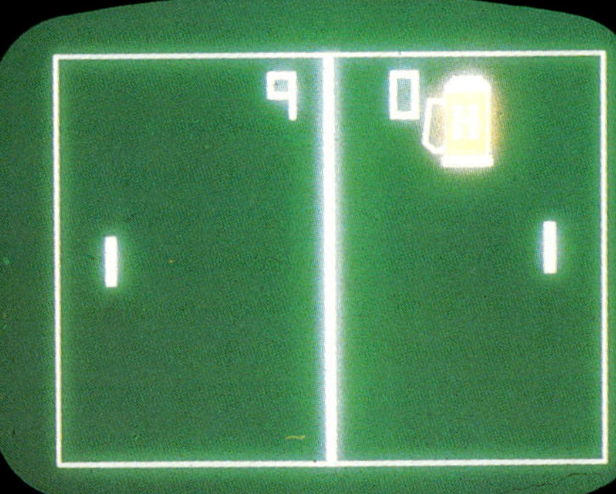

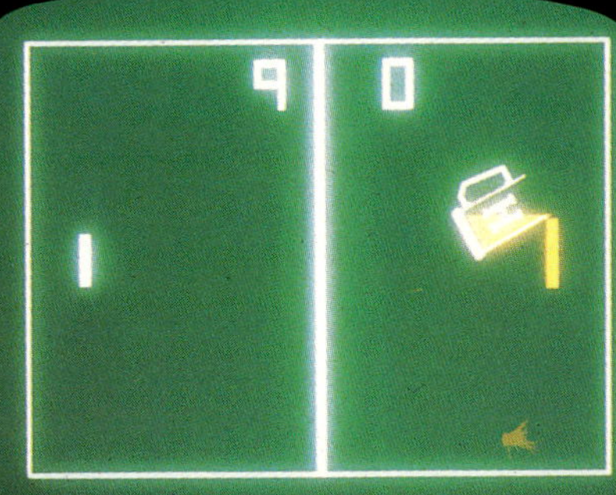

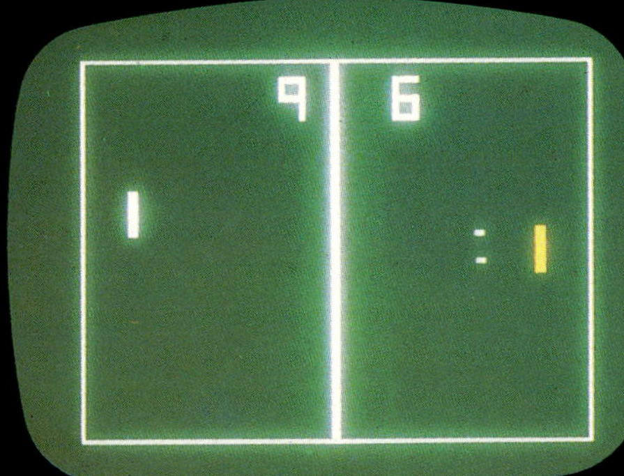

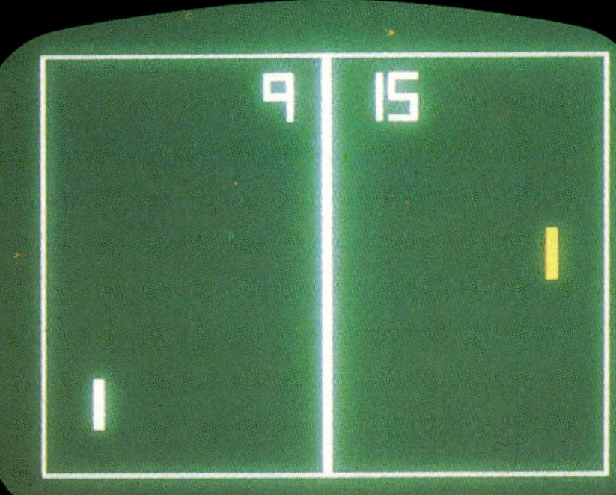

Heineken

Heineken refreshes the parts other beers cannot reach.

"ELECTRIC TENNIS"

Most of the commercials you will see during an evening's viewing are described, optimistically in some cases, as "Live Action" – that is, there are live people moving around in front of the camera.

There is another kind of commercial, closer to science fiction than real life, which comes from the shadowy world of Special Effects – a world inhabited by animators, cardboard engineers, cell retouchers, rostrum camera operators and, quite probably, elves and goblins. If you want the impossible or the non-existent, these are the people to fix it for you. Close your eyes for a moment, and... *abracadabra!*

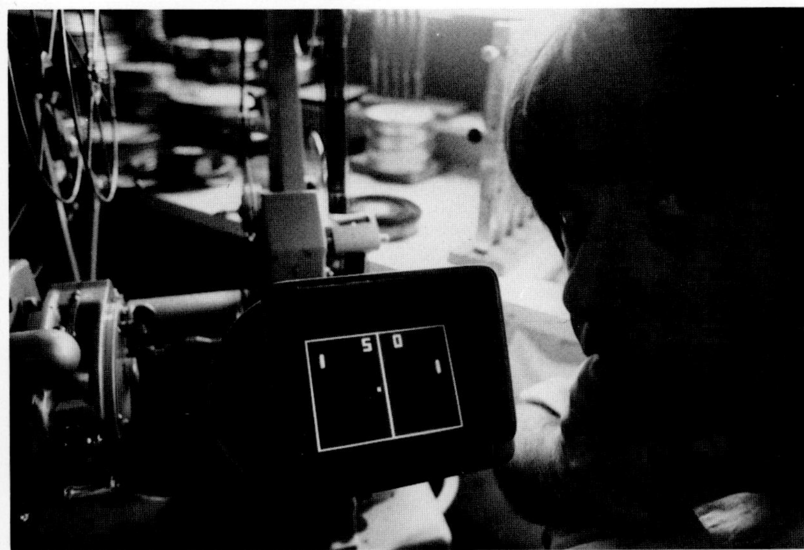

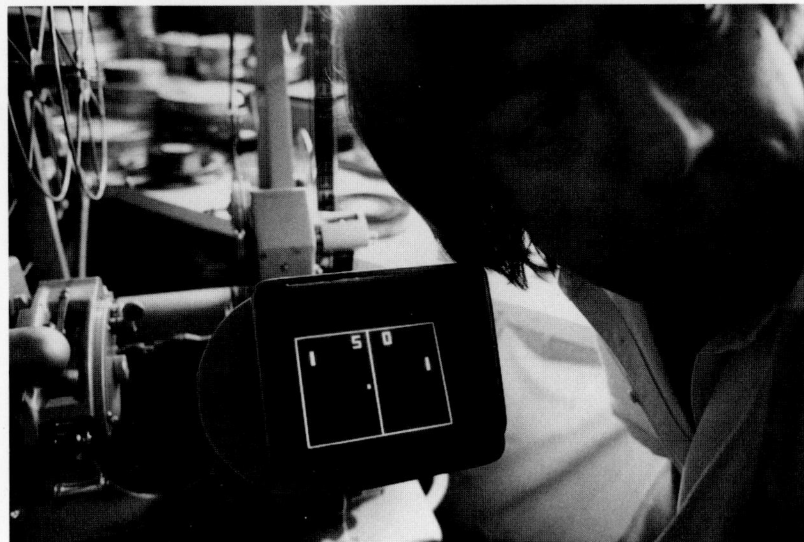

Wonderful stuff. But if you ask the obvious question – how did you do it? – they won't tell you. They might mutter a few spells and incantations, but nothing very revealing. Because despite their electronic gadgets, their laser technology, their computerised animation systems, they are, at heart, good old-fashioned illusionists, magicians, conjurers – and they will never tell you exactly how they got the rabbit into the hat.

Charlie Jenkins, who is responsible for this commercial, did admit to making a model of the game and spending several days with it in a dark cupboard.

How interesting. Then what happened?

Abracadabra!

And with that, he vanished.

'Deckchair'

1980 March

SFX:
'Don't Laugh at Me 'Cos I'm a Fool"
music.

"DECKCHAIR"

Every director has his favourite nightmare. This is Paul Weiland's.

He is on the front at Scarborough, directing his boyhood hero, Norman Wisdom. He is feeling very exposed, because two thousand of Norman's fans – "oooo, isn't he lovely!" – have turned up to watch and offer advice.

Time is running out, and the scene to be shot is a complicated sequence involving Wisdom, a large cast of extras, an obstinate deckchair and, in a small but critically important role, a waiter.

All the waiter has to do is give Norman Wisdom a pint of Heineken and retire gracefully, but this proves too much for him. He tries a dozen times – too soon, too late, too high with the tray, too clumsy with the beer. Norman's fans, realising that all is not well, are silent. The waiter tries once more. No good.

Time, light and patience are now in very short supply, and the waiter is actually getting worse with each attempt. Weiland is desperate, and decides to demonstrate exactly what he wants. He takes the tray and – the eyes of Scarborough upon him – serves the pint. Impeccable! A star is born!

The crowd instantly recognises talent and gives the new waiter a big hand. Someone else gives him a white jacket, the camera rolls, and it's all over.

On the strength of his performance, Weiland has been offered jobs in several Italian restaurants and a season at Butlins but, for the moment, he is staying behind the camera.

□ □ □

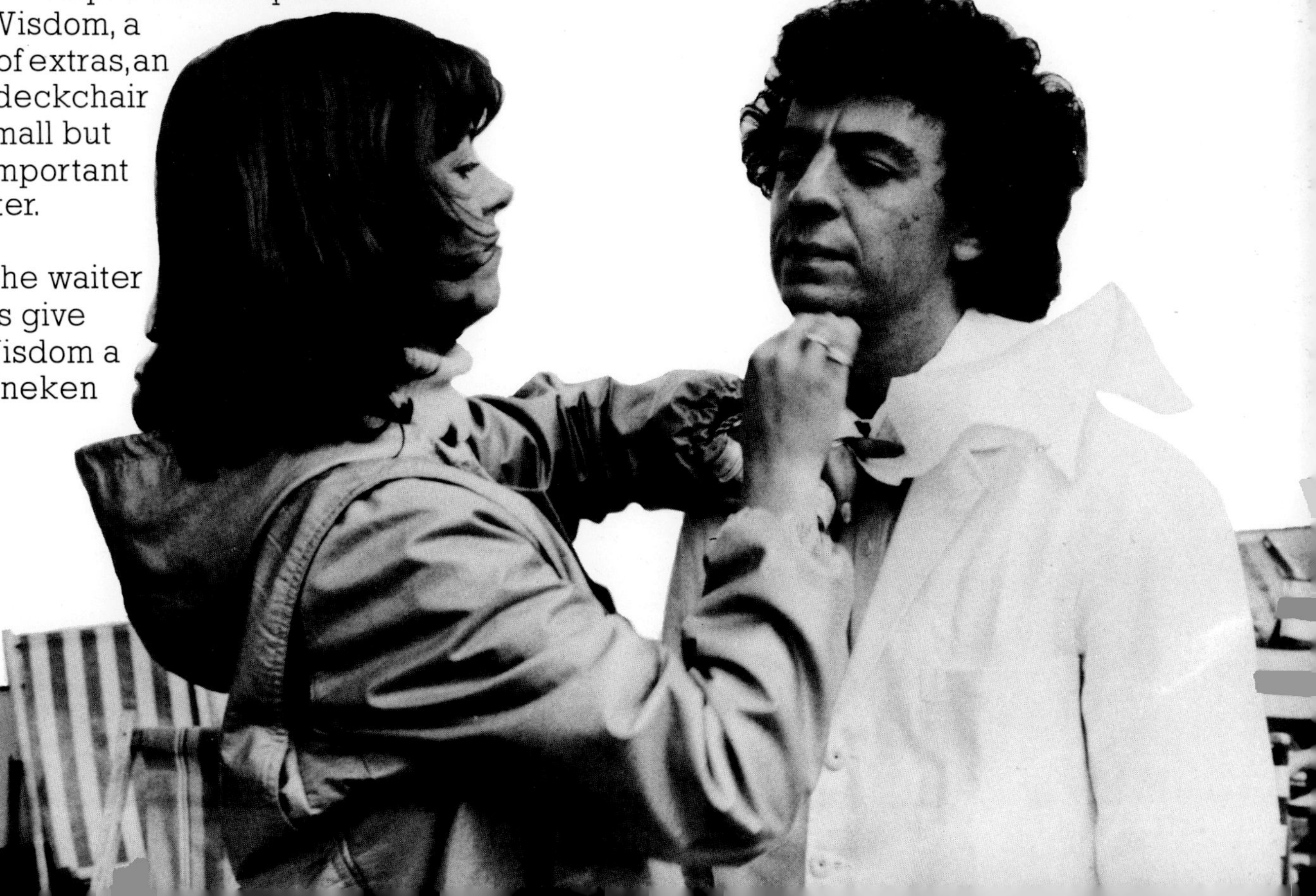

'Windermere'
1982 May

MUSIC:
Romantic throughout.

SFX:
Nib on paper, writing.

VOICE:
I walked about a bit on my own…

SFX:
Nib on paper, crossing out.

SFX:
Nib on paper, writing.

VOICE:
I strolled around without anyone else…

SFX:
Nib on paper, crossing out.

SFX:
Can opening and drinking.

SFX:
Nib on paper, writing.

VOICE:
I wandered lonely as a cloud that floats on (fading) high o'er vales and hills.

VOICE:
Only Heineken can do this because it refreshes the poets other beers cannot reach.

□ □ □

"WINDERMERE"

In 1804, nature was a lot more reliable than it is today. A man could go up to the Lake District in early spring and be sure to find daffodils. Not one or two miserable specimens, but a *host,* all tossing their heads in sprightly dance and inspiring a rush of poetry to the pen.

But what do we find now? Conflicting and untrustworthy reports from the daffodil spotters. This week? Next week? The week after? Surely by the week after. They're *always* out by then.

And, of course, when you get up there with the crew and the cameras and the actor and the equipment, there isn't a single daffodil to be seen. Can't understand it, say the daffodil spotters; they're *always* out by now.

Well, we can't hang around waiting for nature. Call London – that's the place for daffodils. Get six thousand of them up here as quick as you can. (Wordsworth saw ten thousand "at a glance," but poets tend to exaggerate.)

Two pantechnicons, stuffed with daffodils, arrive at the location. Dibbers are issued all round, and the crew, the agency people, the pantechnicon drivers and one or two passing hikers are put to work planting.

As you can imagine, the daffodil spotters come in for some good-natured banter as the backs get stiff and the blister count rises, but eventually a carpet of daffodils – "Continuous as the stars that shine/And twinkle on the milky way" stretches into the middle distance, and our poet can get on with it.

□ □ □

One down, 5,999 to go.

'Onion Seller'
1982 July

SFX:
Music.

SFX:
Faint rumbling.

SFX:
Rumbling gets louder.

SFX:
Horn tooting.

□□□

"ONION SELLER"

The problem is that a bicycle built for six places certain demands on the riders which are at odds with the Gallic character. Not just a highly developed sense of balance, but perfect unison – six pairs of legs moving as one – is required. And perfect unison of any kind has never been a strong point with the French.

Nevertheless, it must be done. The director, Michael Seresin, reasons with them until, humming the Eton Boating Song (which has the ideal rhythm for pedalling) the riders move off, gingerly at first, and then with greater assurance. Well done, *mes enfants!* Let's film it.

Seresin, who is shooting with a long lens from several hundred yards away, now sees through the camera a most disturbing sight: *the bicycle is sinking from view.* As the last beret disappears below the horizon, he runs over to investigate.

All six onion sellers are on the ground, helpless with laughter, pointing at the two ruptured bicycle wheels which have collapsed under their weight. What a brilliant commercial, they tell Seresin. We had no idea we were supposed to fall off. Oh, you English!

There now follows a period of controlled panic while France is scoured for reinforced bicycle wheels and spare six-seater frames. Miraculously, they are found overnight, and shooting starts the next morning with stronger wheels. All goes well.

In Paris, Seresin shows the finished commercial to the actor who played the leading onion seller. He asks why the funny bit has been left out.

□ □ □

'Any road up'
1982 October

SFX:
Traffic and road works.

SFX:
Roll of thunder.

SFX MUSIC:
Singing in the rain.

□ □ □

"ANY ROAD UP"

On the surface, a delightfully simple idea, even though it does combine the two different techniques of Special Effects against a Live Action background.

Once again, we coax Charlie Jenkins – the man who did the Electric Tennis commercial – out of his dark cupboard. Can we persuade him to break the illusionist's vow of silence and tell us how this one was done?

All right. First of all, you make this black plastic peel-off man, an exact replica of the official road sign symbol, and you stick him on a specially made blank triangular road sign, and you film it. Got that? Right. Then you somehow have to replace that image with the animated figure that does all the business with the pint and the umbrella and the little dance.

But if we did a straightforward substitution, there would be a visual hiccup; the eye would notice the change. So what we have to do is provide a distraction while the substitution takes place, and an appropriate distraction is a flash of lightning. The plastic man, under cover of the lightning, becomes the animated man. Got that? Right. Well, after that it's simple, isn't it? Don't need to go through all the technical details. They'll just confuse you. And now, for my next trick...

□ □ □

'Boomerang'
1980 May

SFX:
Didgereedoo music and S/Fx throughout.

□ □ □

"BOOMERANG"

Commercials are normally safe enough as long as you keep away from power cables and those lethal sausage sandwiches. But there are odd occasions when danger lurks on every side, and this is one of them.

It all starts quietly, with our man in the outback throwing his boomerang collection into the distance. He is observed by a passing wallaby. (As a rule, one isn't too keen on working with animals because they're so unpredictable, but this wallaby looks like a steady fellow.)

And then, some genius has a bright idea: why don't we – this'll make them laugh – why don't we put the cold Heineken in the wallaby's pouch? And – *this is really priceless* – we'll slip three pounds of ice cubes in there as well.

Now put yourself, if you can, in the wallaby's position. Hopping around a studio is one thing; it makes a day out from Pet's Corner at Whipsnade. But a can of beer and three pounds of ice cubes *in your pouch!* Without drawing any vivid and indelicate comparisons, you can imagine how that must feel. Would it encourage you to look with affection on your co-star, or would you want to kick him, with your spring-loaded back paws, in the same direction as his boomerangs?

So with a vengeful wallaby in the background, our hero now has to turn and face a firing squad. It's the crew, armed with boomerangs which they are returning to sender. Ten, twenty, thirty boomerangs hurtle towards him. The wallaby, maddened by melting ice cubes, waits behind him. And an even more perilous commercial lies in store for him, as we will see on the next page.

□ □ □

Do you mind a few ice cubes in your pouch?

'A real charmer'

1983 April

VICTOR:
Here we witness a centuries old Eastern tradition. The Indian snake charmer.

CHARMER:
Mutters to himself.

VICTOR:
Normally he could charm the birds out of the trees. But today he cannot even charm the snake out of the basket.

Fortunately help is at hand or rather on head. The cold Heineken.

Immediately our friend is his charming self once more.

SFX:
Music.

VICTOR:
Oh dear, not those two again.

Well, I suppose it only goes to show Heineken still refreshes the parts other beers cannot reach.

"A REAL CHARMER"

Three years have passed, and the boomerang scars have healed nicely, when the call comes. Another Heineken commercial? Well, it can't be as bad as the last one. What could they possibly want me to do that's worse than that?

Nothing to worry about, so the director says. (It's that ex-waiter, Paul Weiland, again.) We just want you to stay in this basket until your cue, then pop up, catch a boomerang – only the one boomerang – and get down inside the basket again. Easy.

That's all?

Well, you have to share the basket.

Who with?

Well, it's a wallaby. But it's all right – it's the same one you worked with before.

No! Not him again!

It'll be fine. There'll be two animal handlers there as well as you and the wallaby.

Three men and a wallaby? In one basket?

Well, it's a good sized basket.

But the wallaby still blames me for all that ice in his pouch! He nurses a grievance! He has *very powerful* back legs!

You'll be all right. Give him some peanuts. At least you're not sharing the basket with a snake. They're *really* nasty.

Thanks.

□ □ □

T.V. COMMERCIAL LOWE & HOWARD-SPINK

189 BROMPTON ROAD LONDON SW3

CLIENT: Whitbread
PRODUCT: Heineken
DATE:

TITLE:
DIRECTOR: Hugh Hudson
LENGTH: 40 seconds

VIDEO

AUDIO

"CALL THAT A COMMERCIAL? I COULD DO BETTER MYSELF"

Each year, as the evenings draw in and the nights grow cold, we see the emergence of a nocturnal, highly vocal species. It nests in front of the television set, uttering scornful cries during each commercial break: "Rubbish! Look at that! Call that a commercial? The bloody cat could do better than that."

Yes, by his song shall you know him (or her). It is the harbinger of autumn, *Scriptus Domesticus*, the amateur advertising writer. Everyone, as is well known, can write better advertising than the people who work in advertising.

And now – opportunity knocks! – here is a chance for one of you to put our money where your mouth is. Using the almost blank sheet of paper opposite for inspiration, write a Heineken commercial, send it with a stamped addressed envelope to Frank Lowe (whose address is at the top of the almost blank sheet), and hold your breath.

All entries will be judged by a fiercely critical panel. The winning idea will be filmed and shown, in peak viewing time, for all the losers to enjoy. And it will be directed by the man who made long running shorts fashionable in "Chariots of Fire," Hugh Hudson. He had just finished directing "Greystoke," and he is beginning to worry about his next challenge. Put him out of his misery. Send in a brilliant idea. Fame and fortune (in very small amounts) could be yours.

□□□

Hugh Hudson and friends at the set of Greystoke.

The Posters.

If you run an advertising agency, one of your constant problems is keeping the creative people, the writers and art directors, out of mischief. This is particularly difficult during that vacuum between the end of one job and the beginning of the next. These people are like one of Wellington's elite cavalry squadrons – magnificent in war and a damn nuisance in peacetime – and you leave them to their own devices at your peril.

In their idle moments, you might expect them – artists that they are – to occupy themselves with slim volumes of verse or visits to the Tate Gallery. Not a bit of it.

They will either disappear for hours on end taking elaborate and costly lunches and listening to tempting propositions from rival agencies ("we'll throw in a Bentley Mulsanne *and* a Filipino houseboy"). Or, *and maybe worse,* they will stay in the office.

And how will they spend their days? Lollygagging, distracting their colleagues, making phone calls to Los Angeles, drinking port, savaging the furniture, insulting the accountant, placing the tea lady in compromising situations, and generally having fun.

But you must bear with them! They are the geese and, from time to time and with prodigious groans of effort, they will discharge golden eggs, gems of memorable and pointed prose, graphic images that become world-famous and sometimes even valuable (try to buy an Alphonse Mucha beer poster for less than £7,000) – yes, given time and encouragement, they will earn their keep.

But what can we do with them in between jobs? How can we save them from their tendency to wretched excess?

Give them stimulating work, an artistic challenge, the chance to be a modern Mucha! At the first sign of restive behaviour, get them to do some Heineken posters.

Over the years, dozens of creative people have produced hundreds of poster ideas for Heineken. The winners appear on the following pages.

It started as a beer poster and turned into an investment.

July 1974

August 1974

July 1975

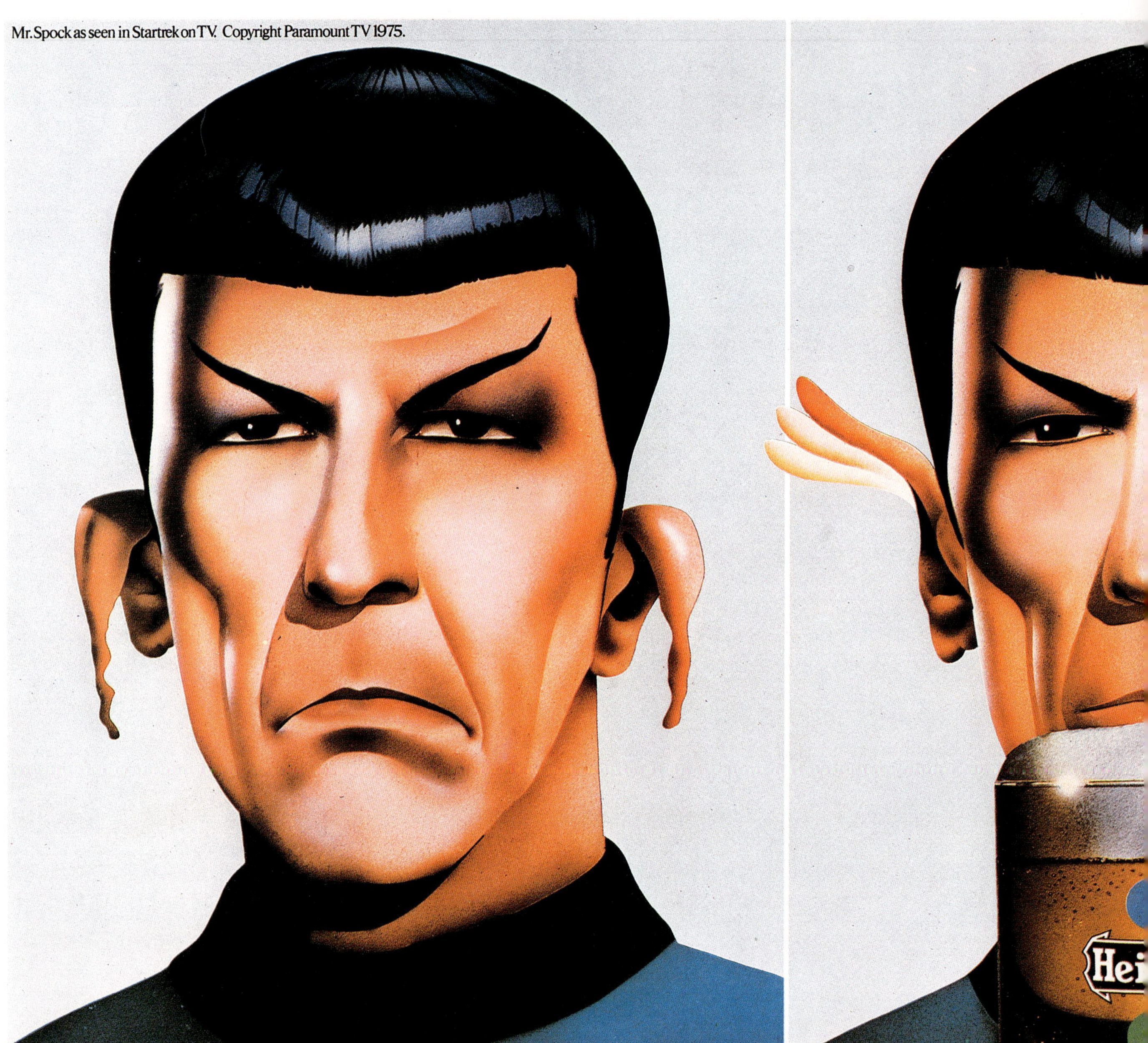
Mr. Spock as seen in Startrek on TV. Copyright Paramount TV 1975.
Hei
Heineken. Refreshes the pa

September 1975

Heineken. Refreshes the parts other beers cannot reach.

August 1976

Heineken refreshes the parts other beers cannot reach.

January 1976

June 1977

December 1977

Heineken. Refreshes the pa

ts other beers cannot reach.

June 1976

Heineken. Refreshes the pa

s other beers cannot reach.

April 1976

Heineken refreshes the parts other beers cannot reach.

April 1978

Heineken refreshes the parts other beers cannot reach.

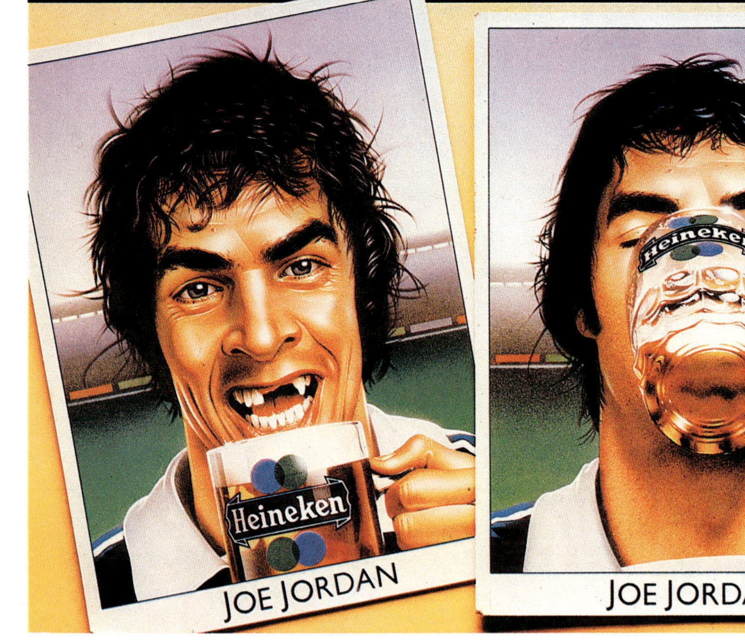

May 1978

June 1978

July 1978

December 1978

March 1979

June 1979

Heineken refreshes the parts other beers cannot reach.

July/August 1979

Heineken refreshes the pa

other beers cannot reach.

July 1980

Heineken refreshes the parts other beers cannot reach.

December 1979

March 1980

Heineken refreshes the parts other beers cannot reach.

August 1980

Heineken refreshes the parts other beers cannot reach.

December 1980

Heineken refreshes the pa

s other beers cannot reach.

July 1982

August 1981

December 1981

March 1982

March 1983

1st December 1982

7th December 1982

14th December 1982

21st December 1982

Heineken refreshes the pa

other beers cannot reach.

April 1983

Heineken refreshes the pa

s other beers cannot reach.

May 1983

Heineken refreshes the pira

s other beers cannot reach.

August 1983

We interrupt the advertising to bring you the news.

It is generally accepted as a bonus, in advertising terms, if your campaign is flexible enough to accommodate the occasional news story.

The theory, which is difficult to argue with, is that news is more interesting than advertising. "Man Bites Dog" will usually attract more attention than "Washes Even Whiter." It follows that if you can take advantage of borrowed interest and, in the manner of a racing driver, slipstream in behind the news, your message and your product should be noticed far more than normal.

The type of news story is irrelevant, as long as it suits your product; you don't have to wait for a Coronation, or an outbreak of harmony in the House of Commons. Any story, however fleeting or frivolous, will do – as long as it's absorbing the nation's attention at the time. Thus we find in the following pages such strangely assorted subjects as the mating of two pandas, the salvaging of a 16th century warship, a royal engagement, and an illicit soap opera romance. All they have in common is that, for a time, they were front page news. And when you turned the page, the chances were that you would see a Heineken advertisement.

Fleet Street has frequently returned the compliment. Newspaper headline writers and cartoonists have adapted the slogan for their own use, and refreshed parts have been seen in the most dignified newspapers. Who are we to complain?

□ □ □

"It refreshes the parts other fuels cannot reach!"

Neatness and order come to the Tate Gallery bricks.

The maiden flight of the Concorde.

The stranded shark, unstranded.

Heineken
Heineken
Heineken. Refreshes the parts
other beers cannot reach.

The Daily Express becomes a single-seat paper.

The freak year 1976, when Britain had a real summer and the ancient art of rainmaking enjoyed a brief comback.

Red Adair and the North Sea Fire Brigade do their stuff on a blazing rig.

A suitably bald comment on the opening night of "The King and I."

The vicar who shot birds, disarmed by the cold Heineken.

Heineken.
Refreshes the parts other beers cannot reach.

Heineken finds its way into Starter's Orders on the day of the Grand National.

The day the Sunday Times returned to the breakfast table after an enforced holiday.

Celebrating That Engagement.

BEST WISHES CHING-CHING AND CHIA-CHIA.

HEINEKEN REFRESHES THE PARTS OTHER BEARS CANNOT REACH.

Over the years, no pun has been left unturned, except perhaps a reference to the bruin business.

THE SUN, Tuesday, June 15, 1982 9

HOW LAGER REFRESHED BILL'S DUFF SPARE PART

KIDNEY-TRANSPLANT patient Bill Hockaday's operation seemed a tragic failure until he downed a drop of the stuff that reaches the parts no othor beer can.

By MARTYN SHARPE

Five weeks after his transplant Bill, 29, still hadn't reached the vital recovery stage—a trip to the loo

He tried everything. Orange juice, Vimto, tea water . . . but nothing worked.

And it looked as though the kidney would have to be removed because of rejection.

Then Bill's wife, Sue, 26, brought him a couple of lagers to cheer him up, as he relaxed at home in Denton, near Manchester.

Within the hour the Heineken wonder brew had done the trick—saving Bill from another operation and a return to the dialysis machine.

Sue said yesterday: "I didn't look at the brand—but when we saw what it was we couldn't stop laughing!"

A much-relieved Bill added: "It may have been coincidence but I'll always put it down to the lager.

Laugh

"I had never even drunk the stuff before—but from now on it's my favourite tipple."

A spokesman for Heineken said: "Our claim is really tongue-in-cheek but perhaps now we will have to take it more seriously."

Bill's doctors at Manchester Royal Infirmary are delighted and amused.

(Beats taking the pils, eh?)

Astonishing medical breakthrough No. 1–Heineken comes to the aid of a kidney transplant patient.

Heineken refresca las partes que otras cervezas no pueden llegar.

The mug salutes the World Cup.

The maestro's coat-tails, as they appeared in a Victor Borge concert programme.

THE SUN, Tuesday, December 15, 1981

LAGER CURE REFRESHES A SILENT POSTMAN

By MURIEL BURDEN

SPEECHLESS Roger Graves has got his voice back . . . thanks to the lager that refreshes the parts other beers cannot reach.

Roger, a 49-year-old postman, was struck dumb a year ago when he caught the parrots' disease, psittacosis.

Doctors despaired as he struggled to speak again. But after a quick gargle in the pub, Roger suddenly found he could chat as well as ever.

He said yesterday: "Losing my voice was sheer hell. I'm a chatterbox by nature, but I couldn't get a word out.

"I had to write everything down on a pad. I got so frustrated at not being able to speak I was taking it out on everybody.

Roger yesterday . . . "losing my voice was sheer hell."

Hospital

"I don't know how my wife put up with me."

The disease, similar to pneumonia, left him with a cough, which in turn made him speechless.

It finally put Roger, of Rownhams Road, Maybush, Southampton in hospital — where he was told to mouth nursery rhymes.

He said: "They told me to whisper Baa Baa Black Sheep over and over.

Tipple

"I was so fed up I went for a drink. I had a lager, came back, tried again and there it was—I could speak."

The tipple dumbstruck Roger chose was Heineken — the lager that advertisements claim refreshes the parts other beers cannot reach.

"That pint certainly did the trick," he added.

"I couldn't believe it. I thought I was doomed to stay silent forever."

We're Speechless.

Heineken

Astonishing medical breakthrough No. 2 – Heineken cures the postman with parrot's disease.

HEINEKEN REFRESHES THE STARTS OTHER BEERS CANNOT REACH.

26 miles to the pint. Is this a record?

HEINEKEN REFRESHES THE PARTS OTHER BEERS CANNOT REACH.

Joking apart, funds are still needed for this historic venture. If you would like to refresh the coffers, please send a cheque to the Mary Rose Development Trust, Old Bond Store, 48 Warblington Street, Portsmouth PO1 2ET.

With dazzling versatility, Heineken helps the Mary Rose to surface, and an errant Russian submarine to submerge.

НЕIИЕКЕИ ЯЕГЯЕЗНЕЗ ТНЕ РАЯТЗ
ФТНЕЯ ЪЕЕЯЗ САИИФТ ЯЕАСН.

Try a pint, Ken. It just might work.

It did.

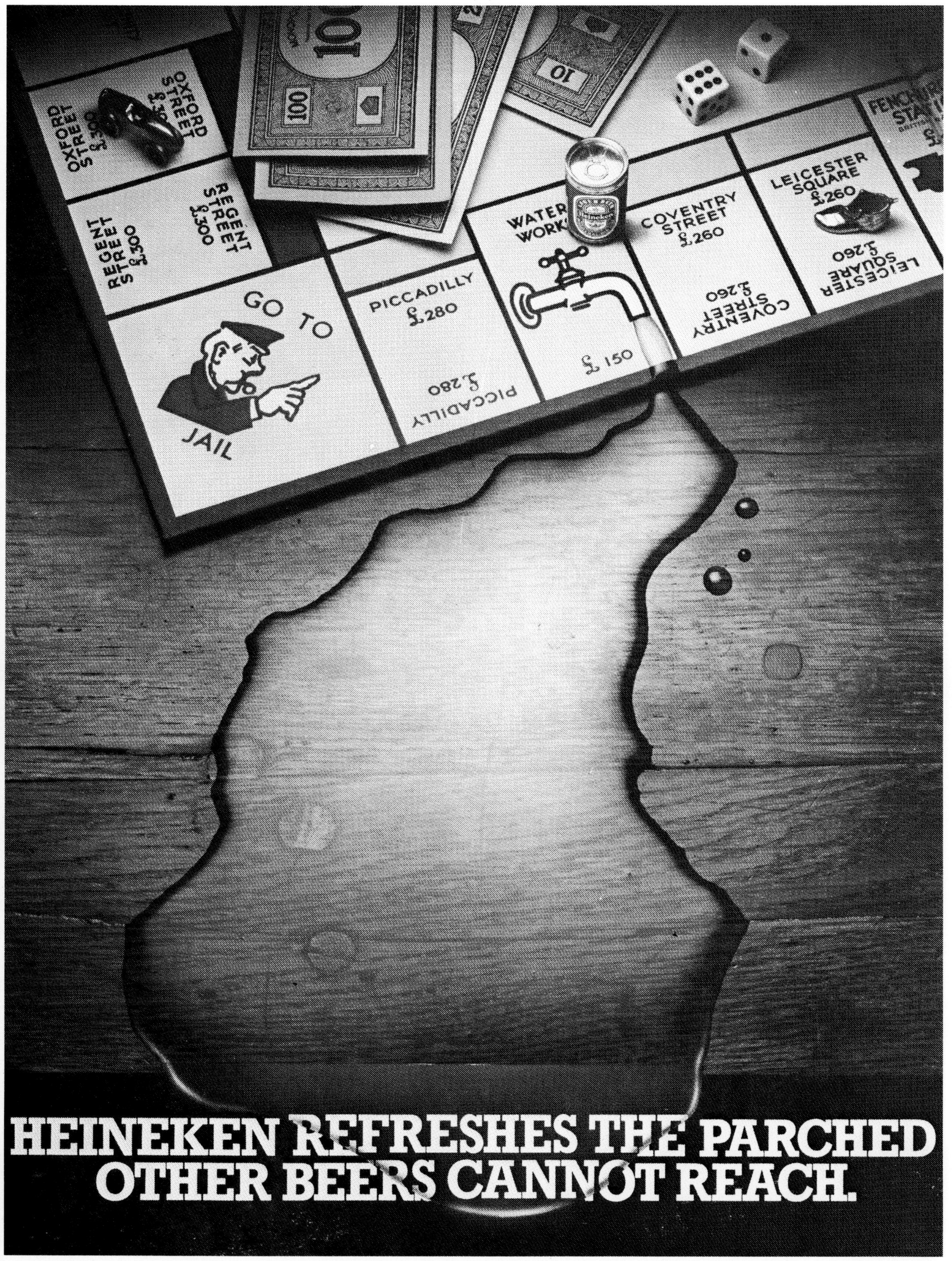

The end of the water strike.

DAILY EXPRESS Monday October 18 1982 7

FROM RONNIE REAGAN TO THE MARY ROSE, HUMOUR MAKES THE WORD GO ROUND

Laughter refreshes the products other ads can't reach

Adding a giggle . . . Cinzano and Heineken humour

Will you be as fortunate finding a second career?

Albany Life

Assured of success . . . President Reagan's ex-movie career triggers a smile

By ELIZABETH GRICE

WE ARE high above the Atlantic at 600 miles an hour. The super sophisticated Joan Collins is, unfortunately for her, sitting next to the super bumbling Leonard Rossiter.

There is much talk about his favourite tipple, the seat recliner button is pressed . . . and a generous glassful ends up over Miss Collins.

We cut to the unfortunate Hobbses, Arthur and Minnie, played by the two Ronnies, are trying to explain to a group of uncomprehending Spaniards that they want to hire a car on the cheap.

Smile

Arthur mimes, beeps, broom-brooms to no avail, while Minnie whimpers on the sidelines. The scene degenerates into Latin chaos, as we are shown a much cleverer couple, the Cholmondley-Pughs (the two Ronnies again) cruise effortlessly to their hotel in a Hertz car.

No prizes for guessing that these are not trailers for a new comedy series but popular television commercials. Cinzano and Hertz are two of a growing band of companies who want to sell with a smile and win consumers with wit.

The British public rightly resists the hard-sell. Those in the business agree that we enjoy our advertising more than any other nation. We enjoy watching Felicity Kendal make an endearing fool of herself in Hotpoint-Schreiber kitchens. We revel in the spectacle of Eric Sykes covering himself in grime in front of a Creda washing machine.

Just how influential you can be these days with a jolly slogan and a witty jape was illustrated last week by Prince Charles and Roy Jenkins. Roy, of course, was extolling the SDP (it reaches parts the other parties can't reach) and the Prince of Wales was praising the little boat that took him close to the wreck of the Mary Rose (it got him to the parts that other boats couldn't reach).

Both of them gave Heineken lager an enormous indirect plug—even if the Eurocrats in Brussels are considering banning the famous slogan under stringent new advertising rules.

However, the ad agency which has the Heineken account, Lowe and Howard Spink, has found the allusion very refreshing.

Spice

Lowe and Howard-Spink is a young agency which spices a large percentage of its advertisements with humour. Frank Lowe, then with Collett Dickenson Pearce, created not only the early Heineken "refreshing the parts" ads but teamed up Collins and Rossiter for Cinzano, stimulating a new market for the aperitif among young people.

The firm's creative director, Alfredo Marcantonio, believes that if you say something with humour, you are more likely to make it stick. "The British have a great reluctance to be sold-to, but they like to be amused. Advertising only works if it informs or entertains. Humorous ads make people feel good about the product."

The same basic theory — make them laugh and they'll feel friendly towards the product—lies behind Young and Rubicam's audacious new Smirnoff ads on the London underground. They are nothing whatever to do with Smirnoff, but they show a series of Marc cartoons with a topical thrust. Overbearing tart confronts potential client: "Fancy some flexible rostering, dearie?" Missing Persons police department suggests to worried inquirer: "Have you tried the Barbican?"

There, stuck in a corner, below the caption, is the Smirnoff label. . . .

Sour

Chris Wilkins, creative director of Y and R, explains: "It is giving people a smile, sponsored by Smirnoff. The joke does not have to be about Smirnoff. It's the fact that Smirnoff are paying for it that rubs off to the benefit of the brand . . . it has made them a small gift of a cartoon."

Some advertisers believe that Saatchis have been responsible for the fact that so much advertising now wears a broad grin. Saatchi executive Simon Mellor makes no grand claims but agrees that more and more firms are realising that "brands have a personality and that it is part of their job to make that personality appealing. Humour can be very useful. It enables you to say tough things without leaving a sour taste in the mouth."

But Saatchis are wary of using well-known comedians, fearing the "vampire video" syndrome, as it is known in the business. This means that the personality gets in the way of the product and is remembered long after the memory of the product has faded.

Saatchi and Saatchi prefers oddbal casting — and there could hardly be an odderball than J.R. of Dallas, who is used in a brilliant current advertising campaign for Dunlop. J. R. Ewing is synonymous with oil. Dunlop's tyres "that save petrol" are a threat to him an[...] best not to reco[...] indeed, to supp[...] that Dunlop [...] tured any such [...]

As joke adv[...] this is about as [...] a genre as we have—the anti-product advert. Dunlop are delighted with it. "I only wish we could spend more money on this kind of thing," said Graham Stanley, the company's advertising manager.

With the joke ad, the anti-product ad and the ad in which everything seems to go wrong, the British appear to have found a happy vehicle for their own peculiar brand of wry, self-deprecating humour.

Take, for instance, the video recorder ad in which a customer insists he must have a *Japanese* model "with all the fiddly bits" even though he can't tell a video machine from a washing machine. Not to be out-done, the sales assistant for Philips pronounces the firm's name "*Firrips*," Japanese-style.

Slogan

But the British were not first with this humour. Bill Bernbach, the inspired American ad man whose agency is famous for such slogans as Volkswagen's "Think small" and Avis's "We're Number 2, so we try harder," used humour as a way of being *almost honest* about a product.

Bernbach died a few days ago at the age of 71, but his legacy is obvious.

Last week, Lowe and Howard-Spink burned the midnight oil to produce an advertisement which showed a fisherman hauling up the Mary Rose, fortified by Heineken lager.

And Collett Dickenson Pearce used the Mary Rose's lifting cradle to "raise" a packet of Benson and Hedges in the great ship's hull. The funny-peculiar and the funny-ha-ha combined to make something typically funny-British.

Not all advertising moguls agree that ads are getting funnier, however. Chris Wilkins, who produces some of the cleverest, suggests that in a recession they actually become more serious. But there is another theory. It is that television is getting duller, so the advertisements appear funnier and that when life is grey the hoardings and the magazine adverts look colourful . . . Can't these ad men treat anything *seriously* any more?

BEER REFRESHES THE FISHES THAT OTHER ANGLERS CAN'T CATCH

Sunday People Reporter

SEA angler Brian Taylor has a novel way of hooking the fish other anglers can't catch.

His secret? Dipping his bait in Heineken, the lager that refreshes the parts other beers can't reach.

Brian, 34, of Paignton, Devon, has smashed two world records with his revolutionary method.

He said yesterday: "It started as a joke one day last July when I was fishing for shark and getting nothing.

Monster

"So I told my mates I was going to dip my bait in Heineken.

"Then I hooked a monster — a 382 lb porbeagle shark, the heaviest ever caught on a 16 lb line.

"I had to play it for 2½ hours before landing it.

"Then last week, using Heineken for the first time since July, I got a 16 lb 15 oz pollock on a 6 lb line, smashing the record set in 1978 by 14 ounces."

Brian, who owns a carpet shop, added: "I know this is hard to swallow, but it's no fishy tale. It really does the trick."

Another Chesterfield champ

SO CHESTERFIELD, that Derbyshire town with an uncanny knack of making champions, has another to add to its list.

Ten years ago, John Lowe was invited to have a game of darts with the lads at the local.

Title

This year, as a full-time professional, he should make £25,000 and might even make £50,000.

Last November — a week after turning pro—this 31-year-old former self-employed joiner, won the World Masters title.

Now he is at the top of the board, so to speak. He's part of a boom in the taproom sport fast removing its image of flat caps and rolled fags.

"I am fortunate," he says, "because I have no nerves when I get on the stage. If you get the shakes at this game, you've no chance.

"There is a lot of money to be made. In August, for instance, they are sending me to America."

It is a tournament in Long Beach, California, with prize money of £55,000."

Some darts players need a drink. One former champion, I am told, couldn't play before eight pints and seven trips to the gents.

Cans

Lowe keeps within limits. 'If I am playing a morning match, I just take a couple of cans of lager."

You know the one . . . it refreshes darts that other beers cannot reach.

AGENCIES RISE TO THE MARY ROSE

THE MARY ROSE drama inspired two agencies to react swiftly with very timely advertisements yesterday. Heineken, who now has a "topical" tradition to maintain, produced a bold fisherman sketch by artist Bob Wilson for ad agency Lowe and Howard-Spink. With the help of Heineken the fisherman pulled up the prize Tudor warship. The lager's famous slogan also got an unexpected free plug from Prince Charles yesterday. Using a very small boat to get close to the Mary Rose he explained: "It gets to the parts other boats can't reach—like the ad."

VICTOR BORG

WIMBLEDON victor—Sweden's Bjorn Borg. He got to parts of the Centre Court Ilie Nastase couldn't reach! REPORT PAGE 35.

If you drink too much there's one part that every beer can reach.

Your health isn't the only thing which suffers if you over-drink. A night of heavy drinking can make it impossible for you to make love.

And even if you think your drinking isn't affecting you, have you ever wondered how it might be affecting your partner?

Put it this way. How would you like to be made love to by a drunk?

The Health Education Council. **Everybody likes a drink. Nobody likes a drunk.**

No comment.

Renaults reach the parts other cars cannot reach.

Everyone of the 35 cars in the Renault range is front-wheel drive. So when snow brings the country to a halt, the Renaults keep going.

And the Renault driver gets into work. In style. In comfort. On time. Renault prices start at £3,199 and end around £10,000. Take a test drive at one of Renault's 500 dealers today. You have nothing to lose but your snow-chains.

RENAULT

elf lubricants.

The sincerest form of flattery.

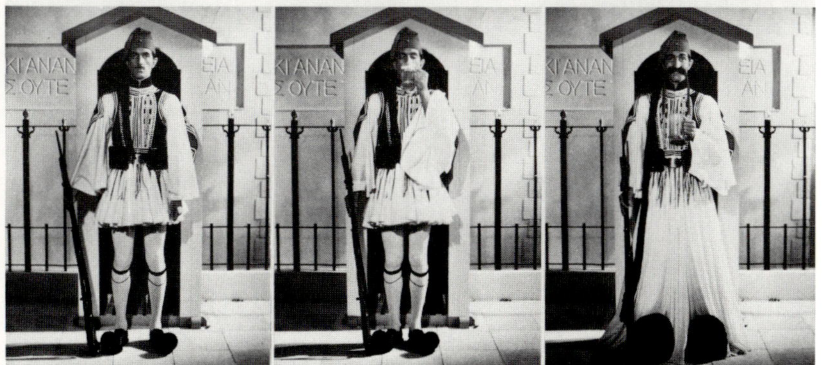

—UNPUBLISHED SUBMISSIONS—

Creative people in agencies, who have a fondness for the unprovable claim, like to say that their best work – the really brave, outrageous stuff – is always rejected. This is never the result of any misdirection of creative effort, but timidity in high places. They were scared of it!

True or not, it's a comforting thought on a Friday night after you've had a week's work turned down.

In fact, advertising tends to operate on the iceberg principle. For every advertisement or poster or commercial that surfaces in public, there are nine that remain submerged. They are rejected for all kinds of reasons, and they are often interesting in the same way that a writer's notes are interesting – they give you some idea of the process which leads to the finished piece of work.

Here are just a few of the poster ideas that never became posters.

In a brave attempt to bring a smile to Coronation Street's most impassive face, this poster idea was presented to the makers of the programme. They laughed, and turned it down, but asked if they could keep a copy of the poster rough. There's no business like show business.

reach.

Laughing all the way to the pub.

Despite a fair amount of evidence to the contrary, the belief still persists that there are two different kinds of advertising, and never the twain shall meet.

The first kind is "selling" advertising. It assumes an almost complete lack of intelligence on the part of the public, and takes the line of attacking the lowest common denominator. To have any effect – like water torture – it requires a high level of repetition and thus a high level of expenditure.

The standard excuse for this kind of advertising is that it won't win any awards, but it will certainly sell the product. There is little sympathy for the argument that better advertising might sell more of the product at a lower cost.

In the opposite corner, we have the distinctive, and sometimes very amusing advertising which assumes that the public has a sense of humour and can grasp words of more than two syllables. This is described by its detractors, with a faint curl of the lip, as "creative" – as though it were an unpleasant affliction. The standard criticism is that it is easier to make people laugh than it is to get them to spend money.

The Heineken advertising, when it first appeared, was classified – or condemned – as "creative."

Good for awards. Bad for sales.

However, nobody had told the public how they were supposed to react. Instead of just laughing, they went out and bought the beer as well.

In the ten years since the campaign started, more than one hundred brands of lager have been launched. Heineken sales in Britain have increased by three hundred per cent and they still continue to grow every year. There are, obviously, many other factors that influence sales – distribution, price, changes in taste, even the weather – but the advertising cannot escape without taking some credit.

□ □ □

SALES

"Five million pints please, Mr. Heineken. And have one yourself."

The man behind the table is Mr. Freddie Heineken. As you might gather from the name, he is also the man behind the beer, and he has worked in the family business for forty years.

During this time, Heineken the beer has become the fourth biggest-selling brand in the world, with sales of about five million pints a day, and Heineken the man has been kept, as he says, "fairly busy."

There have been a few spare moments, however, to add to his various collections. There is the Heineken collection of cars, of houses, of languages, and – from one-liners to minor monologues – the Heineken collection of jokes. They come flying at you in Dutch, in French, in German, in English, in sign language – in between comments on business management, design and advertising, and the finer points of brewing lager.

It's just as well there is a healthy sense of humour in the chairman's office in view of the possible social consequences of the advertising slogan. Just think if it were your name up there on the posters and commercials. There's no escape from it! You're at a cocktail party, in a restaurant, checking into a hotel – *nowhere is safe* – when suddenly, at the sound of your name, someone who can't resist the opportunity turns to you and says: "So *you're* the man who refreshes the parts..."

Grin and bear it! It is, after all, a result of the effectiveness of your own advertising philosophy: if a good product and a sound strategy are the hops of beer advertising, then a sense of humour provides the yeast. Incidentally, have you heard the one about the three men in a pub? No? Well, perhaps another time.

□ □ □

David Thorpe.

TEN YEARS LATER

The advertising business feeds on change. Clients change their agencies, agencies change their names and their staff, big agencies spawn little agencies, today's great idea is elbowed aside in the rush for tomorrow's even greater idea, and, with one eye on the future and the other eye looking warily over the shoulder, a frantic time is had by all. It is not, in other words, a business noted for stability or long-term associations. Campaigns and people come and go – *let's have something new!* – with giddy speed.

And yet, ten years later, here we see the old firm of Simonds-Gooding and Lowe, late of Leningrad, minus the fur hats and plus a few grey hairs, but still taking care of things. A rare and, we might say, refreshing change.

An advertising campaign does not last for ten years by accident. Forces are at work all the time to dilute it or send it careering off in a different direction. It needs to be defended from that arch-enemy of all good advertising, the committee. It needs to be shielded sometimes even from the well-meaning attentions of marketing experts, art directors, writers and film directors – all of whom want to make their mark, and whose eagerness to improve the idea can often nudge it off course. It needs to be nursed through shifting market pressures and social conditions. And it needs, above all, a constant supply of disciplined enthusiasm to keep it fresh and contemporary.

Not always easy. There are periods, not of boredom exactly, but staleness. Is the idea getting jaded? Has it worn itself out?

Henry Ford, so the story goes, was reviewing an advertising campaign with his agency, and said that he'd seen it so many times that it made him sick. But Mr. Ford, they said, it hasn't started yet. An extreme case, certainly, but it serves to illustrate the point that even the sponsors of the advertising are not immune from that nagging voice: *let's have something new!* More often than not, the nagging voice wins and the advertising suffers.

Finally, an aspect of the campaign which only became evident in the course of preparing this book. Heineken advertising has been fun to work on, and the people involved are proud of the work they have done. That doesn't happen very often. And never by accident.

Gentlemen, you deserve a drink.

□ □ □

Bailey.

Simonds-Gooding and Lowe.

APOLOGIES AND ACKNOWLEDGEMENTS

In a musical chairs business like advertising, it is not easy to establish whose bottom was on which chair at any given time in the past. When the past extends back over ten years, the task becomes almost impossible.

Consequently, although we have done our best to give credit where it's due, there may be some errors and omissions. If there are, we apologise.

The people who were involved in the work that appears in this book are listed here.

□ □ □

THE ACCOUNT EXECUTIVES

Michael Cane
Barry Cox
David Gray
Geoff Howard-Spink
Alan Howe
David Jones
Ian Schoolar

THE COPYWRITERS

Derek Apps
Tony Brignull
Gerard Edmondson
Mike Everett
Adrian Holmes
Andrew Imrie
John Kelley
Alfredo Marcantonio
Pete Mathews
Linda McDonald
John Salmon
Geoffrey Seymour
John Silver
Ray Skellorn
Steve Spence
Chris Street
Paul Weinberger

THE ART DIRECTORS

Gary Campbell
Dave Christensen
Eddie Floyd

John Foster
David George
Dave Horry
Pete Ibbottson
Tony Kaye
Zelda Malan
Rob Morris
John O'Driscoll
Arthur Parsons
Nigel Rose
Paul Smith
Vince Squibb
Mike Stephenson
Anthony Stileman
Kevin Thomas
Alan Waldie

THE ILLUSTRATORS

Alan Aldridge
Bristow
Mick Brownfield
Philip Castle
Barry Craddock
Bill Dare
Paul Davis
David Engle
Oscar Grillo
Mark Hess
Guy Hodgkinson
JAK
Larry
Luck & Flaw
James Marsh
Reg Smythe
Mike Terry
David Wilcox
Bob Wilson

THE PHOTOGRAPHERS

David Bailey
Jack Bankhead
Alan Brooking
Elliott Erwitt
Phil Jude
Reid Miles
Phil Marco
Gerry Oke
Jimmy Wormser

THE DIRECTORS

Bob Brooks
Bruce Brown
Ross Cramer
Vernon Howe
Hugh Hudson
Charlie Jenkins
Tony May
Alan Parker
Mike Seresin
Paul Weiland
Roger Woodburn

THE TV PRODUCERS

Annie Alexander
John Cigarini
Ronnie Holbrook
Judy Hurst
Erika Issitt
Peter Levelle
Barbara Levett
Alan Marshall
Alec Ovens

THOSE WHO WORKED ON THE BOOK

Terry Bailey
Dave Beer
Brian Hill
Steve Hobbs
Tim O'Neill

LAST BUT NOT LEAST

All the people at the brewery – too numerous to list here, who have worked on Heineken over the years. Cheers!

Heineken